Lektürehilfen

T. C. Boyle

The Tortilla Curtain

von Karl Erhard Schuhmacher

Klett Lerntraining

Karl Erhard Schuhmacher, Gymnasiallehrer für Englisch, Geschichte und Sozialkunde in Rheinland-Pfalz; Fachleiter für Englisch.

T. C. Boyles Roman *The Tortilla Curtain* (New York: Penguin und Klett, 2004) liegt unter ISBN 3-12-573840-7 mit einem 19-seitigen Vokabelanhang als Klettbuch vor. Auf diese Ausgabe bezeihen sich die Seitenangaben der Lektürehilfe.

9 783129 230015

Bibliografische Information der Deutschen Bibliothek
Die Deutsche Bibliothek verzeichnet diese Publikation in der Deutschen Nationalbibliografie; detaillierte bibliografische Daten sind im Internet über http://dnb.ddb.de abrufbar

Auflage 8. 7. 6. 5. | 2014 2013 2012 2011
Die letzten Zahlen bezeichnen jeweils die Auflage und das Jahr des Druckes.

Internetadresse: http://www.klett.de
Umschlagfoto: dpa Picture-Alliance GmbH (dpa)
Satz: DTP Andrea Eckhardt, Göppingen
Druck: Beltz Druckpartner GmbH & Co. KG, Hemsbach
Printed in Germany
ISBN 978-3-12-923001-5

Contents

Picture Credits

S. 5: Corbis/Gail Albert Halaban – S. 18: Avenue Images/Corbis – S. 20: David Bacon – S. 23: Topanga Historical Society – S. 48: Keystone – S. 80: Jim Huber – S. 106: Yahoo – S. 107: Corbis/MAPS.com

I The Author

"First look at him: 6 feet 3 inches tall and built like a pencil. Relaxing at home, he wears a black leather jacket over a black T-shirt with a school of fish painted on it, and baggy grey pants. His hair, the color and consistency of soapy steel wool, tufts out at the side of a black beret. His mustache and goatee are nearly Mepistophelean."
(Bruce Weber, "Novel Appeal", *New York Times Magazine*, 1989)

1. The Making of a Writer

Tom Coraghessan Boyle was born on December 2, 1948, in Peekskill, a small town situated on the east bank of the River Hudson in New York State. The settlement was founded in the 17th century by the Dutch merchant Peeck and became to be known as Peeck's kill or Peekskill in English (with "kill" meaning *brook* or *creek*). T.C. Boyle is like many of today's Peekskill residents of Irish ancestry. His parents on both sides are Irish. At the age of seventeen Boyle replaced his middle name John which he was given after his father by Coraghessan, an Irish name of one of his mother's ancestors. His father who grew up in an orphanage became a bus driver; his mother was a school secretary. She used to read newspaper stories out to him – a fact which Boyle is grateful for.

Growing up in the 1960s meant to him – as to many of the young people of the hippie and protest generation – a troublesome process, the more so as both his parents suffered from alcoholism. In early childhood he enjoyed playing all kinds of ball games (baseball, basketball and football), but as he grew older, "rebellion kicked in, in earnest. He played drums and the saxophone, sang in a rock band, drank, took drugs, drove the local roads like a lunatic" (Bruce Weber, "Novel Appeal", *New York Times Magazine*, 1989). Boyle attended Lakeland High School in Shrub Oak, Peekskill, and graduated from it in 1964 with low grades.

> "I was a kid like any other kid. […] Held my own in school, as though it was like servitude. I was a good kid, I tried to please – as children of alcoholics so often do – and yet somehow, at fifteen or sixteen, I metamorphosed into a wise guy. A punk. A cynic. A know it all. Partly, books were to blame – but not fully, not quite yet. The people I ran with – kids, that is – were the children of educated parents, middle-class and even wealthy parents, and they were sly, smart, and disaffected. Later there would be drugs, but at first there was the only desperate-to-get-laid maniacal driving, the usual acts of vandalism, liberated booze – and somehow, miraculously, books. We were proto-hippies, but we didn't know it. We just knew we were caught somewhere between the hoods and the honor students and that we had a taste for Aldous Huxley, George Orwell, J.D. Salinger, Jack Kerouac" (T.C. Boyle, "This Monkey, My Back", 1999).

In 1965 Boyle enrolled at Potsdam College, State of New York University, with music as his only option for a major. When he failed in his audition, his interest in music faltered. Instead, he entered creative writing classes where he and his lecturers discovered his literary talent. He switched to an English and History major, and in 1968 he graduated with the lowest possible grade. "I was a poor undergraduate. I didn't attend classes and hung out with the losers" (T.C. Boyle, "This Monkey, My Back"). But in spite of his complete lack of academic ambition in his undergraduate years he then experienced a literary revelation.

> "I didn't really think about the power of literature until I read the short story 'A Good Man is Hard to Find' by Flannery O'Connor. That's the story that really woke me up to what literature could do. I must have read that story over one hundred times now. It still scares me and makes me laugh at the same time" (Jack Rightmyer, "T.C. Boyle Says Books Saved His Life", *Daily Gazette*, Albany 2003).

To avoid being drafted into the army and sent to Vietnam after leaving college in 1968 Boyle went back to his former high school to teach English. Lakeland High School had meanwhile become a troublespot and, as a teacher joining such a school, he was exempted from the draft. But he could not cope with the climate of aggression and drug addiction at his old school, which seemed completely changed to him. He suffered much in classes, he often lost his nerve and even attacked some of his students physically.

> "This was a very tough slum school, mainly black and Puerto Rican. I had to rip their shirts, throw them against the wall, get physical. [...] At the same time this was when I started to get into heroin and hang out with all those people. So I was up all night stoned, and I had to go in and do this job. It just about killed me." (De Curtis/T.C. Boyle interview, in: Markus Schröder, *Nice Guys Finish Last*, p. 17)

In spite of his desperate mood and psychic disorder Boyle started writing short stories in earnest and succeeded in publishing his first story "The OF&Hepatitis RR or Bust" in the *North American Review* (1972). This was a pivotal event for Boyle's further life and career. On the merit of this story he was admitted to the University of Iowa Writers' Workshop in 1972. There he was privileged to be taught by famous writers like John Cheever, John Irving and Raymond Carver. At the same time he was admitted to graduate studies in English literature. In 1974 he acquired his M.F.A. in 19th century English literature. He then sternly pursued his academic career: With a collection of short stories written as a dissertation he succeeded in gaining a Ph.D. in literature (1977). This collection was published two years later as his first book titled *Descent of Man and Other Stories* (1979).
It is amazing how Boyle managed to transform his formerly unstable life and stick to unwavering self-control once he set foot in Iowa. Aged 25, he abandoned the apathy, disorder and low expectations of his Peekskill years. He developed great assiduity in classes, displayed perseverance, self-discipline and steadiness.

> "When I went to Iowa [...] I knew that this was what I wanted to do and I was a great graduate student. I got my Ph.D. and I am very proud of the fact that while I was a screw up prior to this, now I got a perfect 4 point through all of graduate school. [...] I had a few very rocky years, and it was part of this hippie culture and drug culture. But I grew up." (Robert Birnbaum/T.C. Boyle, "Robert Birnbaum Talks with the Author of *Drop City*", 2003)

In 1977 Boyle married his long-time friend Karen Kvashay whom he had met at Potsdam College and who had accompanied him to Iowa.

2. A Writer Making it

During his Iowa years Boyle avidly and intensively read works of English and American literature. He felt drawn to texts "with a certain black humor, leaning toward the absurd" (Jared Friedland, "Black Humor, Leaning Toward

the Absurd. An Interview with Author T.C. Boyle," *Education Update Online*, May 2004). Besides the lasting effect of Flannery O'Connor's short story "A Good Man is Hard to Find" Boyle cites John Barth, Thomas Pynchon and also Evelyn Waugh's 1934 novel *A Handful of Dust* as influences on his writing. They "showed Boyle the profound effect a writer can achieve by inverting the tone of a piece from comedy to horror. It's a technique the young author quickly assimilated, and one that has come to characterize much of his fiction, from short stories like 'King Bee' to his 1998 novel, *Riven Rock* (Jared Friedland, "Black Humor, Leaning Toward the Absurd. An Interview with Author T.C. Boyle," *Education Update Online*, May 2004).
Boyle maintains that the main thing a writer has to concentrate upon is to write a gripping story. "Literature is a living, brilliant, great thing that speaks to you on an individual and personal level. [...] I think the essence of it is telling a story. It's entertainment. It's not something to be taught in a classroom, necessarily. To be alive, to be good, it is to be a good story that grabs you by the nose and doesn't let you go till The End" (*Meet the Writers: T.C. Boyle,* Barnes and Noble, 1999, www.Barnesandnoble.com). But all the same Boyle's novels are structurally and aesthetically crafted very skillfully. They display depth in the depiction of human behavior and, in fictional, often satirical disguise, address urgent social, economic and environmental issues. In addition, all of Boyle's works excel in verbal exuberance, irony and wit. They "crackle with the flamboyant energy of a ferocious, delicious imagination, often darkly satirical and always infatuated with language" (*Los Angeles Times*, quotation from the cover of T.C. Boyle, *Without a Hero*, Granta Books 1998).

In the late 1970s Boyle moved to Los Angeles together with his wife Karen. They first lived in a small canyon settlement of Tujunga (L.A.) among bikers and rednecks. After some time they moved to Woodland Hills (L.A.) which from Topanga is "just over the hill", as the natives say (see map, p. 106). Their Woodland Hills residence exuded solid respectability. Visiting friends of old mocked at the incompatibility of Boyle's still eccentric outer appearance – remains of his rock-and-roller and punk years – and the spacious middle-class home with soft, tufted red-leather couches in the living room, a silver service on the dining-room table and a swimming pool out back (cf. Paul Ciotti, "The Hemingway of the Hudson", *Hudson Valley Magazine*, December 1987). One day Boyle was stopped by the police who suspected him of car theft judging from his outer appearance which seemed somehow not bourgeois enough to fit in with the red BMW that he was driving (cf. Bruce Weber, "Novel Appearance", *New York Times Magazine*, 1989).
In 1978 Boyle accepted the post of Assistant Professor in the English Department at the University of Southern California, Los Angeles. His success in establishing thriving creative writing classes there prematurely earned him the position of Professor of English in 1986. In the early 1980s he wrote the

novels *Water Music* (1981) and *Budding Prospects* (1984) as well as his second collection of short stories *Greasy Lake and Other Stories* (1985). In 1988 Boyle celebrated his national and international breakthrough with his third novel *World's End* which is set in the Hudson area around his hometown Peekskill (in the novel featuring as "Peterskill") contrasting colonial past and present. This book won him the prestigious PEN/Faulkner Award for the best US novel in 1988.
In the mid 1990s Boyle and his wife bought and restored a house built by the famous architect Frank Lloyd Wright in Montecito, a suburb of Santa Barbara. They left Woodland Hills because of the population pressure to live there. The success of his books and the money gained from the movie *Road to Wellville* allowed Boyle to make this privileged move. In spite of his outstanding literary and economic success he has maintained his post at the University of Southern California and still commutes the 100 miles to Los Angeles to conduct his courses there. "I love teaching. [...] I get a rush out of helping young people with their writing. It makes me feel great to help them and give back some of what I know" (Jack Rightmyer, "T.C. Boyle Says Books Saved His Life", *The Daily Gazette*, Albany 2003).

Meanwhile Boyle has become a writer of international status. *The Road to Wellville* (1993) has been turned into a movie, and *The Tortilla Curtain* (1995) will shortly be filmed starring Kevin Costner and Meg Ryan as Delaney and Kyra. *Drop City* (2003) and *The Inner Circle* (2004) – published as *Dr. Sex* in Germany – have become international bestsellers. Boyle's humor and biting irony, his exuberant verbal power, his great imaginative power to create such differing characters as the adventurer Mungo Park, the health guru Kellog, the 17-year-old pregnant América and, lately, the sex expert Dr. Kinsey, and last but not least his gift to write a gripping story – all this makes readers worldwide eagerly wait for 'the new Boyle'. His talent of lively performance in his lectures and of making a public reading an event, his willingness to go on lecture tours all over the world, his pleasure to indiscriminately take up contact with everybody (see the TCB forum on Boyle's website TCBoyle.com), his well-preserved image of a former drop-out and rock-and-roller, his flamboyant appearance – all this singles him out as an extraordinary literary figure with immense popularity.

Life and Works: A Chronology

LIFE

- Born on December, 2nd 1948 in Peekskill (New York State)
- Graduation 1964: Lakeland High School, Peekskill
- B.A. (1968) in History and English at Potsdam College of State University New York
- M.F.A. (1974) University of Iowa: 19th century English literature
- Ph.D. (1977). As a dissertation Boyle submitted his collection of short stories *The Descent of Man* published in 1979.
- Professor at the University of Southern California since 1978 (Assistant Professor 1978 – 1982, Associate Professor 1982-1986, Professor of English since 1986)
- He lives in Montecito, Santa Barbara, CA with his wife. They have three adult children.

WORKS

- *Descent of Man*, 1979 (Stories)
- *Water Music*, 1981
- *Budding Prospects: A Pastoral*, 1984
- *Greasy Lake and Other Stories*, 1985
- *World's End*, 1987
- *If the River Was Whiskey*, 1990 (Stories)
- *East is East*, 1991
- *The Road to Wellville*, 1993
- *Without a Hero*, 1994 (Stories)
- *The Tortilla Curtain* (1995)
- *Riven Rock*, 1998
- *A Friend of the Earth*, 2000
- *After the Plague*, 2001 (Stories)
- *Drop City*, 2003
- *The Inner Circle*, 2004
- *Tooth and Claw*, 2005 (Stories)

3. An Easterner turned Californian

We can be sure that with Boyle living and working for 12 years in and about L.A. (1978 – 1990) he became familiar with the place, its nature, fauna, flora, canyons and creeks, its repetitive natural disasters, its society with illegal immigration, crime, urbanization, overpopulation, pollution, traffic congestion, day laborers, gated cities and their residents. With Topanga as the fictional center, Boyle sets his 1995 novel *The Tortilla Curtain* in his own former backyard. On the other hand, as his workplace, the University of Southern California, is right in the center of Los Angeles and Boyle has now been a faculty member there for 28 years, he is certainly very much aware of the increasingly explosive situation in the inner city area of L.A. (crime, race-

related riots, car thefts). And, of course, he knows of the desperate financial situation of the city.
When in 1995 his readers were confronted with *The Tortilla Curtain*, many of them were irritated by its uncommon seriousness. They did not expect the author to tackle California's most burning political and social issues, namely illegal immigration, urban sprawl, crime, gated cities and social inequality. Some people even doubted Boyle's qualification to deal with Californian problems. Others questioned the authenticity of his writing characterizing Mexican day laborers from an internal perspective. "Who the heck does this middle-class white dude think he is to write about this stuff as if he knows about it? What makes him think he can write about being Mexican, let alone an illegal immigrant?" So the deliberately provocative question put by an interviewer playing the devil's advocate. But Boyle seeems to have overcome his first indignation about people questioning his competence as a writer and now stresses the fact that he has lived in this conflict-laden area with open eyes for quite some time. In addition, he expresses his long-standing concern for Mexico and the Mexicans:

> "It may sound silly, but I've always felt an affection for Mexico and Mexican culture. I grew up in New York, as you may know, and the language I studied from 8th grade on was Spanish. [...] Even before I moved to California I had traveled in Mexico and Central America. When I decided to write this book, I knew that I had to see one thing only. And that was the fence there. So I went back to Tijuana. [...] And it's a real war zone, it's a real disaster, Tijuana, let me tell you" (*Penguin Reading Guide*, "T.C. Boyle Interview", see Appendix 4).

II The Background of the Novel

1. The U.S.A. in the 1980s and 1990s

1.1 Economic Aspects

For many Americans the years of the Reagan Administration (1982–1988) were an economic boom time. Tax cuts, deregulated business, low inflation and a revival of private entrepreneurship led to a flourishing economy and to great wealth for the upper strata of society. The ideology of the so-called neo-conservatism favored individual responsibility as well as free economic growth and limited the government's influences on economic and social affairs. But for those at the bottom of the social ladder these years meant hardship and even neglect, the more so as the ever-growing budget deficit did not allow for any substantial social programs. Each year the government had to pay 150 billion dollars in interest on the national debt which amounted to 3 trillion dollars by the time Reagan left office in 1988.

In the 1980s 15% percent of the population lived below poverty level, which is a rise of 3.5% against the 1970s. A former Carter aide wrote in 1986: "The evidence grows steadily stronger that we are building a class-ridden society of ever-sharper contrasts between haves and have-nots" (DiBacco et al., *History of the United States*, p. 824). At the same time Reagan was capable of awakening a new patriotism and an optimistic belief in the uniqueness of the nation and the strength of its citizens.

George H. Bush (U.S. President from 1988 to 1992) struggled hard to follow the road of successfully cutting state expenditure in order to bring down the budget deficit. A substantial turnabout, however, came with President Clinton. He managed to virtually eliminate all the debts of the federal budget and to achieve a solid economic growth which was based on low unemployment and low inflation rates, and fuelled by the booming stock markets and revolutionary technological progress in computer industries, microelectronics and communication. This era (1992–2000) allowed a great majority of Americans to enjoy job security and rising incomes.

1.2 Immigration and Demographic Change

The new immigration law of 1965 ended the old quota system which in the past had favored European immigrants. Having left behind the traumatic experience of the failure in Vietnam the newly shining U.S.A. of the 1980s and

1990s with its renewed faith in ever-increasing economic and social improvements presented a strong attraction to immigrants all over the world. The 1980s and 1990s have seen a **soaring growth in the number of immigrants**, surpassing the historical wave of the turn from the 19th to the 20th century. In the decade from 1990 to 1999 the total number of immigrants reached the all-time high of about 9,1 million, topping the peak years of the first decade of the 20th century with its 8,8 million immigrants.

U.S. Immigration Level 1961–2000	
Period	**Total Immigration**
1961–1970	3 321 677
1971–1980	4 493 314
1981–1990	7 338 062
1991–2000	9 095 417

Source: Statistical Yearbook of the Immigration and Naturalization Service (INS)

More important than the rise in absolute numbers is the fundamental change in the ethnic **patterns of immigration**: Since the late 1960s there has been a massive decrease of European immigrants, a tremendous increase of Hispanic immigrants from Latin America and of Asian immigrants. Mexico has been the largest single contributor to American immigration. Today 20 % of the immigrants now living in the U.S.A. are Mexican-born.

Foreign Born by Region of Birth: 2002
(in percent)

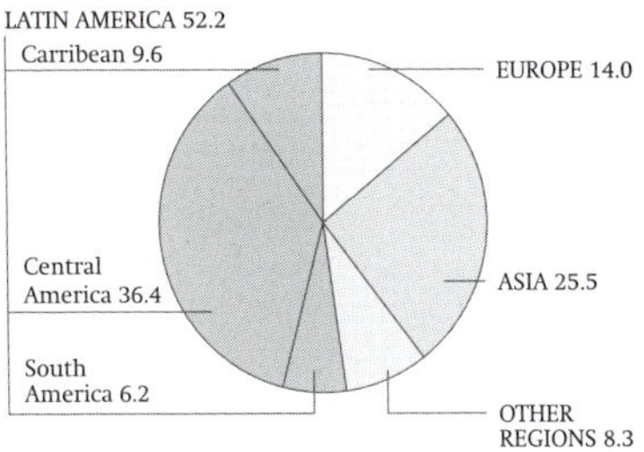

Source: U.S. Census Bureau, Current Population Survey, March 2002

In comparison, in the two decades from 1941 to 1960, 54 % of the immigrants came from Europe, 22.6 % from Latin America (10.2 % from Mexico) and 5.1 % from Asia.

Accordingly, the **ethnic makeup of the U.S. population** has been rapidly changing. By 2000 the Hispanic or Latino population had become the largest minority group with 12.5% of the total population, surpassing the traditionally largest ethnic minority of the African-Americans ("the Blacks") who constitute 12.3% of the U.S. population.

Throughout the early 2000s the Hispanic population grew faster than any other group in the U.S.A.. By 2003 its percentage had risen to 13.4% of the U.S. population with a total of approximately 40 million people. The share of the Asian population has risen to almost 4%.

All non-white ethnic and Hispanic groups together constitute about 30% of the U.S. population. With the undiminished influx from Asia, Latin America and above all Mexico and considering the fact that these groups in contrast to the white Anglo population have much higher birth rates, demographic observers speak of the **"browning of America"**. After each census there are projections showing that **white Anglos will be a minority** in the U.S.A. in the near future.

The regional distribution of the **Hispanic population** displays concentrations in the Southwestern states, in Florida and New York. In some cities, counties and communities the share of the Hispanic/Latino population surpasses all other groups including the non-Hispanic Whites. Here the Spanish language and Hispanic culture (shops, newspapers, radio/TV stations) dominate the scene in local communities.

Share of Hispanic / Latino population (of total population)	
California	32.4%
New Mexico	42.1%
Texas	32.0%
Florida	16.8%
New York State	15.1%
Los Angeles	44.6%
New York City	27.2%
San Fernando, L.A.	89.28%
Topanga	5.08%

Source: U.S. Census 2000

1.3 Dealing with Illegal Immigration

Some of the strain on the social systems of Southwestern border states and cities has been brought about by illegal immigration. Figures based on the Census 2000 show that between October 1996 and January 2000 over a million illegal immigrants entered the U.S.A. raising the total in the country to 7 million. The vast majority of these illegal aliens are from Mexico and most of them live in California.

The Californian Coalition for Immigration Reform (CCIR) drafted an initiative paper which in 1994 was introduced by the Republican state assemblyman Dick Mountjoy as the Save Our State initiative. Its advocates hoped that preventing access to public services such as education and prenatal care to illegal immigrants would stop the flow of undocumented workers from Mexico.

This initiative found its way on the ballot paper of the 1994 November state elections as **Proposition 187**. In the official ballot argument it was described as "the first giant stride in ultimately ending the ILLEGAL ALIEN invasion". Governor Pete Wilson (Republican) was a prominent supporter of the campaign whereas Gray Davis (Democrat), who was to become Wilson's successor in 1998, opposed this proposition. In November 1994 Proposition 187 was passed by almost 60% of Californian voters. They seemed to fear the social and fiscal effects of mass immigration such as an increasing crime rate, a lack of safety, unemployment, depleted public funds in social services, overstrained health care services, deteriorating school education and rising disorder. However, as parts of Proposition 187 were unconstitutional (they encroached upon federal competences), nothing came of it, and the remaining parts were dropped by the Californian governor.

Since the early 1990s corrugated iron fences and walls have been put up along the American-Mexican border. These fortifications under the surveillance of the Border Patrol have come to be known worldwide as the **"Tortilla Curtain"**. In contrast to the former Iron Curtain it is obviously not as solid, for it has not prevented countless numbers of Mexicans from crossing, often under inhuman circumstances. They take the risks of being cheated by unreliable "coyotes" (Mexican scouts who organize and guide the border crossings for money), of being rounded by the Border Patrol and sent back, and of becoming victims of crime. (For further information concerning the "coyotes" see chapter IV, section 7.4.)

The fortification and surveillance measures along the Tortilla Curtain have so far not been successful in curbing illegal immigration. One simple reason for this lies in the fact that half the number of the present 7 million illegal aliens in the U.S.A. entered legally and just overstayed their short-term visas – in the hope of not being found and turned out by the **INS** (Immigration and

Naturalization Service). This government agency has a police-like force trying to detect illegal immigrants nationwide: *La Migra*. But the main cause for the Mexican migration into the U.S.A. lies in the desperate social and economic situation in Mexico and the lure of the affluence in the U.S.A. North America's and specifically California's dependency on cheap labor and the comparatively high wages represent such a strong pull factor that Mexicans are not deterred by any security measures.

Regarding the high overall figure of 7 million illegal aliens in the U.S.A., with many of them living and working there for years, some political observers believe that an amnesty (the second after 1986) has to be granted to those illegal aliens who have been living in the U.S.A. for a minimum of five years and have an unblemished record. It is estimated that this would enable about 5 million people (mostly Hispanics) to leave their shadowy existence of illegalty and to acquire social security and the right to be employed as legal immigrants.

This move is strongly criticized by opponents of mass immigration who believe that "high levels of Hispanic immigration threaten to disrupt the political and cultural integrity of the United States and, [...] that the United States faces the loss of its core Anglo-Protestant culture and may soon be divided into two peoples with two cultures and two languages (English and Spanish)" (Sam Francis, "Immigration vs. 'Anglo-Protestant' America", *Sam Francis Archive*, February 26, 2004).

1.4 Gated Communities

South California and especially Los Angeles have strongly felt the demographic impact of mass immigration. In the last two decades features like overpopulation, urban sprawl, traffic congestion, air pollution, social unrest, and racial conflict have made life there unpleasant – belying the glamorous image Hollywood gives to the city. It is therefore no surprise that those who can afford it have tried to get away from it all and have moved out of the inner city and densely populated urban parts to more pleasant places within commutable distances. Now these people realize that the ever-expanding process of urbanization has reached the outskirts bringing city life with all its ills to their once idyllic retreats.

The Santa Monica Mountains, a range of hills rising up just north of Hollywood and extending for about 50 miles to the northwest, have become very popular as a refuge for L.A. city residents of the middle and upper classes. Spectacular views, great scenery, forests and State Parks, canyons and creeks, rich almost Mediterranean fauna and flora and above all the smogfree elevation of the terrain (up to 700 meters) have attracted people tired of L.A. city life. In the last fifteen years new residential areas, gigantic developments and luxury housing have sprung up sprawling over the hills northwest of

Hollywood, towards Encino, Woodland Hills, Topanga, Calabasas, Malibu, and Agoura. You will also find super-rich people, Hollywood celebrities and even German "Promis" residing there in mansions and castles. Business for the many real estate agents of these communities has boomed in the last decade and it still does. But there is a fundamental change going on.
By now gated communities have spread ubiquitously across the U.S.A. with highest concentrations in Florida and California. Already by the end of the 1980s there existed about one hundred gated communities in the San Fernando Valley, L.A. (see map, p. 107). Hidden Hills, L.A. is a gated community of about 2,000 residents which has seceded from L.A. County and has the status of a completely independent city. T.C. Boyle's fictional Arroyo Blanco development would be categorized as a "retrofitted" gated community whose residents – under the assumed menace of increasing crime – decided to put up gates and walls for self-protection. Gated cities are run by the bodies of the home owner associations (HOAs) which in democratic fashion care for streets, community centers, garbage pick-up, leisure facilities, library, and, of course, safety. Traditional government services like police, fire, sewerage, and water remain with the local government of the city or county. It soon became clear that no protective system whatsoever can rule out crime from outside. Ironically enough, bored teenagers from within the walls became delinquents and threatened the safety of their parents. There is an ongoing heated debate in the U.S.A. about the effects of gated community living on U.S. society and democracy.

Blakely / Snyder, *Fortress America*

- "Gated communities [...] have been springing up around the country since the early 1980s. Millions of Americans have chosen to live in walled and fenced communal residential space. [...] In this era of dramatic demographic, economic and social change, there is a growing fear about the future in America. Many feel vulnerable, unsure of their place and the stability of their neighborhoods in the face of rapid change. This is reflected in an increasing fear of crime that is unrelated to actual crime trends or locations. The phenomenon of walled cities and gated communities is a dramatic manifestation of a new fortress mentality growing in America" (p. 1 f.).
- Since the mid-nineties there is a heated public debate whether any neighborhood should be walled and gated as Americans in all regions are faced with a dramatic rise in the number of gated commmunities. "In fact, new homes in over 40 percent of planned developments are gated in the West, the South and Southeastern parts of the United States" (p. vii).
- "We estimate that more than 3 million American households (with some 8,4 million people) have already sought out this new refuge from the problems of urbanization" (p. 2 f.).

Since Tocqueville's famous analysis of American society and culture it is America's pride that its communities are all-embracing and not socially divisive and that its citizens display great willingness to join community efforts for the good of the community (American "volunteerism"). Many observers fear that the new trend for separation and exclusion will endanger core virtues of American culture, such as democracy, community spirit and social commitment. Some even fear that America is about to lose those ideals that are essential elements of its identity. In the words of Robert Reich, Labor Secretary of the Clinton Administration, the rising number of gated communities constitutes "'the succession of the successful' from their responsibilities in the civic life of broader society" (*St. James Encyclopedia*, entry: *gated communities*).

Topanga has its only gated community in Summit Pointe Estates. When Boyle published *The Tortilla Curtain*, Summit Pointe was under construction or at least very new. It has a man-guarded gate and many impressive homes and mansions in varied architectural styles. There is no "Spanish Mission Style", as Boyle suggests in his novel.

The Spanish Mission style is found almost solely in those states that have a Spanish Colonial heritage. It originated in California during the 1890s and

Old Spanish Mission

was given impetus when the Southern Pacific Railways employed it for the depots and resort hotels the company constructed throughout the Far West. Early domestic examples were faithful copies of their colonial ancestors, but during the first two decades of the twentieth century other influences – most notably those of the Prairie and Bungalow styles – were added to produce new prototypes.

1.5 Day Labor

In the Far West as elsewhere in labor-intensive agricultural areas, Mexicans (and other Hispanics) have traditionally found **temporary work on farms** as legal or illegal **migrant workers**, or as documented guestworkers in the Bracero Program (1942–1964) and later in the SAWS Agricultural Workers Scheme (1980s). In the Far West from Washington State and Idaho in the North down to California in the South, farmers had and still have to recourse to a temporary workforce to have their fruits picked or potatoes and other vegetables harvested.

With the American economy getting into its stride in the late 1980s and early 1990s the labor market asked for greater flexibility also in non-farm jobs. In urban and suburban areas all over the U.S.A. the demand for part-time and temporary jobs grew creating a new niche for the immigrant workforce. Since the mid 1980s exchange sites for **day labor** sprang up rapidly in California. A study of the Los Angeles area reveals that since the mid 1990s about 20,000 day laborers have been daily gathering at about 100 hiring sites in the hope of finding an employer for the day (Valenzuela, "Working on the Margins", p. 1 ff.). Most of the day laborers offering their work publicly are male Mexicans – women are very rarely seen there, although they are not barred from participating in this market. The laborers comprise all age groups from 17 to 75 having a recency of arrival from 'just arrived' to twenty years and more. The picture of Hispanics waiting patiently on street corners and empty lots or home improvement stores has become a common sight in Los Angeles County. Many of the sites have become loosely regulated by public bodies to guarantee some basic order and to meet the demands of residents who complain about noise, litter, traffic obstruction, public urination and drug-related disturbances. In some communities public agencies and humanitarian groups like CHIRLA (Coalition for Humane Immigrant Rights Los Angeles) cooperate to secure safe and community-accepted meeting places where, in addition to orderly hiring procedures, waiting day laborers are offered amenities. Here they can read newspapers, do some gardening, play chess, watch TV and receive advice. Sometimes there are brokers or longstanding day laborers who see to it that everybody gets a fair chance when employers arrive. In other places CHIRLA volunteers organize raffles to allocate the workers to the employers.

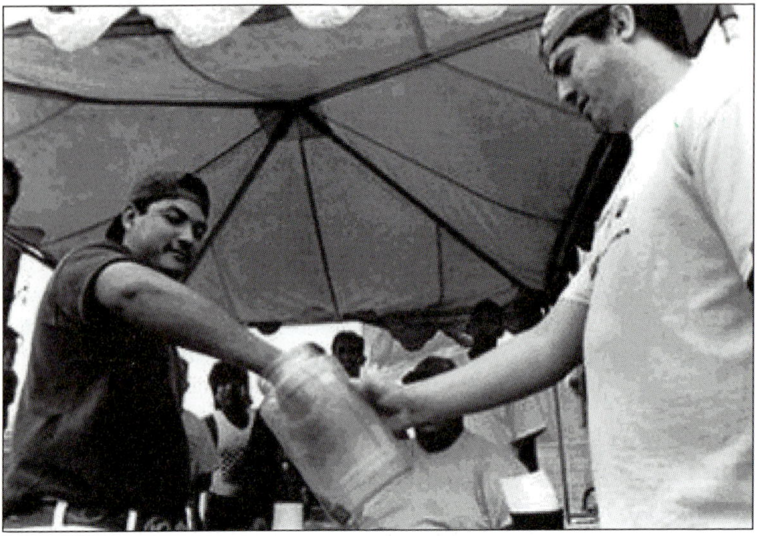

A day laborer draws a name from a jar at the North Hollywood day labor site administered by CHIRLA. The workers use the raffle system to assure that work is distributed fairly among those waiting for work.
Source photograph: David Bacon. Copyright 1990–1999

Private employers benefit from this easy and flexible way of hiring laborers to help them instantly with painting, decorating, building walls, fences, and driveways, reparing roofs, gardening, or clearing sites. There is no paper work, there are no invoices, you just have to have some cash: and, of course, you can cut down on costs as there are no deductions. If as an employer you are dissatisfied with the work, you need not trouble about dismissal and labor rights, you just hire somebody else the next day. Moreover, construction contractors in particular make use of the uncomplicated and flexible method to replace a regular worker or employee who has called in sick. The Los Angeles Study of 1999 arrived at an hourly wage rate of about 6,90 dollars among the 481 surveyed "jornaleros", at that time 1,50 dollars over the federal minimum wage (Abel Valenzuela, "Working on the Margins", p. 12). As day-labor jobs are by their very nature unstable and as earnings strongly depend on seasons, weather, and circumstances, a yearly income cannot be computed on a statistical level. But the study shows "that day laborers who are persistent, competent and assertive can earn a decent living, particularly in the high-demand summer months. Nearly all laborers pay some sort of housing and still manage to send home an average of 2,600 dollars a year"

(Nancy Cleeland, "Many Day Laborers Prefer their Work to Regular Jobs", *Times Mirror Company*, 1999).

Day laborers are usually paid at the end of the day in cash "under the table", i.e. tax-free. Quite a number of them seem to see an advantage over permanent low-pay employment. They may be in a position to negotiate their wages; they enjoy a certain choice in taking up a particular job or not; in most cases no documents are asked for; and if they are met with intolerable work and working conditions, they have the freedom to walk away. Nevertheless, day laborers take considerable risks which they are ill-prepared for. Half of the workers surveyed by Abel Valenzuela complained about cases of having been cheated of their rightful wages at least once; others reported about having to work without breaks or under threats. No worker in the study had a private health insurance, so some of them had encountered hard times after on-the-job injuries as they can hardly afford the storefront medical clinics or even hospitals.

2. The "Mexican Disease"

In the last 35 years Mexico has gone through various economic and political crises endangering the stability of the state and the cohesion of its society. The troubles of 1982 were caused by towering **national debts**. This resulted in a financial state crisis and an economic decline and stagnation for almost a decade.

The reason that there was any growth at all in the early 1990s is to be seen in the tremendous increase in Mexico's population, which more than doubled from 40 million inhabitants in 1960 to almost 95 million inhabitants in 1995. But the first signs of economic and social recovery in 1993 were again crushed by various interrelated events: the Indio revolt in Chiapas in January 1994, the continuing activities of zapatist revolutionary forces in the South and the **dramatic fall of the peso** (50% loss of its foreign value) caused by yearlong **inflation**. Income and wealth inequality rose to a precarious level (in 1994 the top 10% of the population received 41% of the income). Political violence, social tensions and corruption gave rise to public cynicism about government and state incompetence.

It is interesting to note that the wealthy groups of society tried to find protection in **fenced-in communities** as a reaction to the explosive social situation in their country. Legal and illegal immigration to the U.S.A. rose sharply, because migrant seasonal workers again went in great numbers to the Western states of the U.S.A., as if the Bracero Programs were still in action. Apart from the rapid growth of Mexico's population, emigration to the U.S.A. was propelled by the **low wages** in Mexico. (The wages to be found in the United States are at least six times higher than those in Mexico.) It is believed that this exodus has had the effect of a safety valve for Mexico's explosive social situation. The mere opportunity for people to leave and realize their **American dream** has relieved tension in Mexico. Moreover, the money earned and saved by husbands, wives, and youths as migrants in the U.S.A., the money saved, sent or brought back to "their folks" left behind in Mexico is a considerable help to many families there. Mexico's governments seem to condone this exodus as they have been unwilling to control emigration since the end of the Bracero Program in 1964.

We can definitely believe Boyle's Mexican protagonist Cándido and others who maintain that there are not enough jobs in Mexico, although the official unemployment rate in Mexico is – for mysterious and political reasons – comparatively low. To Cándido Mexico is a "country with forty percent unemployment and a million people a year entering the labor force, a country that was corrupt and bankrupt and so pinched by inflation that the farmers were burning their crops and nobody but the rich had enough to eat" (p. 199f.).

Topanga Canyon

III The Story

Part One: Arroyo Blanco

Chapter 1
Delaney Mossbacher – the unwitting perpetrator

Delaney Mossbacher – a nature writer – living with his second wife Kyra and her son Jordan in the Arroyo Blanco Estates, Topanga, Los Angeles County drives up the canyon road of Topanga Park "with a backseat full of newspapers, mayonnaise jars and Diet Coke cans for the recycler" (p. 3). Suddenly his car hits a man who has obviously tried to cross the road "at the last possible moment" (p. 4). Delaney Mossbacher who has never had an accident before is extremely upset by the event. When he sees the man flinging himself across the road, he abruptly stops and stalls the car in a cloud of dust. Although he is sure he must have hit the man, "to his shame" (p. 4) his first thoughts are for the car and for his insurance rates. Only then do his thoughts turn to the victim.
Delaney, the "liberal humanist" (p. 3), slowly realizes that he has injured or even killed a fellow human being. Deeply shocked he gets out of the car, "looks round him helplessly" (p. 4), but cannot see the man either on the road or in the brush alongside. Then he examines his newly waxed Japanese Acura car and finds some damage to the front right headlight. He peers into the brush and the bushes along a trail which steeply falls down the hillside towards Topanga Creek. His car might have catapulted the body over the side of the canyon "like a Ping-Pong ball shot out of a cannon" (p. 6). As nobody gives an answer to his calls, he suddenly feels certain that he has become the victim of a faked accident to be robbed by a gang. But finally he hears someone moaning and finds a badly injured man lying on the ground. Blood leaks from the corner of his mouth, the right side of his face is "raw, scraped and flensed like a piece of meat stripped from the hide" (p. 7), and his left arm grasping his shopping bag is bleeding heavily. Delaney addresses the man offering help. "For a long moment they stood there, examining each other, unwitting perpetrator and unwitting victim" (p. 8). The victim answers in a foreign language Delaney cannot understand. He knows only French and Norwegian, but it soon dawns on him that the man must be a Mexican. Delaney is relieved to see that he is able to speak and move. The Mexican declines Delaney's clumsy and half-hearted offers to help him in any way, but finally manages to ask for "monee" rubbing the fingers of his free hand

together. Delaney gives 20 dollars to the Mexican who grabs the bill and instantly disappears down the trail.
Delaney gets back to his car and drives to the recycling center. His mind, however, is so preoccupied with this unsettling occurrence that he twice goes past it. The image of the injured Mexican haunts him and fuels a feeling of guilt in him. But when he realizes that the Mexican must be camping or even living down in the canyon, intense anger rises in him. As a naturalist and active environmentalist he detests the masses of garbage in nature and the pollution of the creeks. Most of all, he is scandalized at the Mexican's irresponsibility, as in the dry hot Californian climate the canyon is a "tinderbox" (p. 11).
After Delaney has unloaded his household waste into the appropriate receptacles and entered the warehouse with its mountains of cardboard and paper, he notices that the workers there just look identical to "his" Mexican. With "a shock of recognition" (p. 11) he becomes aware for the first time that in Los Angeles you can see the Mexican workforce people everywhere. "Where had they all come from? What did they want? And why did they have to throw themselves under the wheels of his car?" (p. 12). Delaney moved to Los Angeles from the East two years ago and has never really wasted a thought about the many Mexican illegals there.
Without delay he drives to his Acura dealer to have the minor damage repaired. When asked "So what'd you hit – a deer? Coyote?"(p. 13), the high-minded liberal humanist lies and says, "A dog" (p. 13). While the car is being repaired, he phones his wife Kyra, a successful realtor, to tell her about the accident. Before he can explain anything, she fears the worst: Something must have happened to her son Jordan. When she learns the actual facts, she criticizes him harshly for his unreasonable behavior. She is flabbergasted to hear that he has bought off his victim with just "twenty bucks" (p. 15). As some kind of excuse he says: "I told you – he was Mexican" (p. 15).

Chapter 2
Cándido – the unwitting victim

Cándido and his young pregnant wife América, who together left Mexico four months ago, now live in a primitive shelter in Topanga Canyon by the creek. After the accident Cándido can hardly walk down the trail. He is tormented by such extreme headaches and pains that he vomits several times and falls down twice before he finally collapses at the bottom of the path. América finds him lying there when she returns from her journey to Venice where she has in vain tried to get a job as a seamstress. She nurses Cándido as well as she can. As his injuries look really bad, she urges him to go and see a doctor. But Cándido stubbornly rejects this idea for fear of being detected as an illegal immigrant and turned out of the country. He soon falls into

feverish hallucinations and numbed unconsciousness not knowing who and where he is.
Only after two days he slightly recovers from the effects of the severe concussion. He regains his mental power and to the relief of his 17-year-old wife his utterances make sense again. Nevertheless, he is still terribly weak and his injuries decapacitate him for any kind of work. So América insists on going to the labor exchange near the Topanga post office to join the queue of day laborers waiting there to be hired. For Cándido this means a fundamental defeat as a man and husband. He is only thirty-three and unable to earn a living for his wife. Moreover, he cannot keep the promise given to her for a better life in the "North, where it was green and lush the year round and the avocados rotted on the ground, and everyone, even the poorest, had a house, a car and a TV – and now he couldn't even put food in her mouth. Worse: she was going to earn *his* keep" (p. 26). Most of all he worries intensely about her safety. He would prefer not to let her go unprotected into that rough male world outside. But in his weak state of health he cannot achieve anything against América's determination to go and find work.

Chapter 3
The Mossbachers – living high up in the Arroyo Blanco Estates

> "High up the canyon, nestled in a fan-shaped depression dug out of the side of the western ridge by the action of some long-forgotten stream, lay the subdivision known as Arroyo Blanco Estates. It was a private community, comprising a golf course, ten tennis courts, a community center and some two hundred and fifty homes" (p. 30).

Like all the houses in the six-year-old development (p. 167) the Mossbachers' house is in the Spanish Mission style. Delaney Mossbacher, his second wife Kyra Menaker-Mossbacher, and her son Jordan share their home with two matching terriers, Osbert and Sacheverell, and the Siamese cat, Dame Edith. Although four days have passed after his unfortunate encounter with Cándido, Delaney is still much affected by it. Nevertheless, the daily routine has set in again pushing the haunting images of the accident aside. Delaney is a naturalist and an independent freelance writer for the nature magazine *Wide Open Spaces*. As a writer working at home his daily routine means first preparing breakfast for wife and son, then driving Jordan to school and finally writing on his monthly column from 9 to 1 o'clock. Kyra is employed at a real estate agency in nearby Woodland Hills where she is "the undisputed volume leader" (p. 31), i.e. most successful in listing and selling houses. She works obsessively all day and is the chief breadwinner of the family. Delaney has inherited enough money from his parents to be able to lead the carefree life of a writer.

This morning the daily routine works as usual; only the dogs make some unusual prolonged noise in the garden. Suddenly there is a terrible dog's scream "which rose in pitch until it choked off as suddenly as it had begun" (p. 36). Delaney hurries out into the garden to see a coyote climbing over the fence with one of their dogs in his jaws. Immediately Delaney takes up the pursuit, climbs over the fence and follows the coyote into the undergrowth. He can catch a few glimpses of the animal before it finally disappears in the forest high up on the mountain. Here the brush is thicker and Delaney knows that he has no chance of detecting the clever coyote. "It was watching him even now, he knew it, watching him out of slit wary eyes" (p. 38). Delaney picks up a stick and and methodically searches the bushes before after hours he finds the severed paw of Sacheverell. To spare his wife the shock he does not tell her about the death of her much beloved pet. Kyra is strongly attached to her three pets as she has had them for a long time, even before her marriage to Delaney.

In the evening Delaney attends a meeting of the Arroyo Blanco Estates Property Owners' Association which was convened to vote on the erection of a guarded gate at the entrance to the estate. As a liberal Delaney opposes the idea of a gate, but he does not want to join the somewhat radical activists who openly fight against it. The meeting is chaired by one of his neighbors, Jack Jardine Sr. After a few people – among them his other neighbor Jack Cherrystone and the Arroyo Blanco resident Jim Shirley – have spoken on the pros and cons of the gate, Delaney summons up all his courage to present the issue which is on his mind and which he thinks is far more important than the gate. Still full of anger because of the loss of their dog he accuses people of carelessly attracting coyotes with leftover food or pet food in their gardens. Already after his first few words the audience starts to protest aloud against him. Delaney becomes furious and, to impress the audience, he takes out his dog's paw waving it in the air. He is then cut short by the chairman Jack Jardine. Delaney indignantly leaves the meeting knowing that he has made a fool of himself.

Disappointed he sits down just outside the community center. After a while the chairman's son Jack Jardine Jr. comes up to him to ask him about "the Mexican". Jack Jardine Sr. is Delaney's "friend, neighbor, advisor and lawyer" (p. 15); so a few days previously Delaney had gone over to Jack's to confer with him about the accident. While Delaney was telling Jack his story, Jack Jr. was present, lolling on the sofa, and overheard everything. Strangely enough, the 18-year-old Jack Jr. now turns the conversation to the Mexican and wants to know where exactly on the canyon road the accident happened. Delaney is puzzled about this, but nevertheless he tells Jack Jr. about the trail that turns off from the canyon road leading down to the creek.

Chapter 4
Cándido and América – living down and out in Topanga Canyon

Although América is not successful in getting any work on the first day and in spite of Cándido's appeals not to try next morning, she again goes up to the labor exchange. This is in fact just a wall-less shelter built by the American employers in a lot near the post office. There is a headman, Candelario Pérez, who sees to it that no one jumps the queue, that the workers leave the place after midday and that they clean up the trash.

While América is away waiting to be hired at the labor exchange, the pain-ridden Cándido is brooding over his hapless life. América was the four-year-old flower girl at his wedding with her older sister Resurrección who he had married when he was twenty years old. At that time he had just come back to Tepoztlán with a lot of money from a nine months' itinerant working stay in Idaho and Arizona. Their marriage turned out to be an unhappy one. They stayed childlesss and to earn their living he had to leave her every year to look for work in *El Norte*. When he returned home after the seventh season, his wife had left him and was expecting a baby from another man. Cándido's attempt to teach this man a lesson failed; he was beaten and humiliated before the eyes of the whole village. After that he led a miserable life, till many years later he met the then 16-year-old América again. He immediately fell in love with her:

> "She was sixteen and she looked exactly like her sister, only better. He set down a bundle of sticks he was carrying and straightened out his back with an abbreviated twist. 'You're América,' he said, and then he gave it a minute as a car came up the road [...], 'and I'm going to take you with me when I go North.'" (p. 52)

With these thoughts Cándido falls into a feverish sleep sweating enormously. He awakes because of his great thirst, but finds their bottles with the boiled water empty. In his despair he drinks the polluted water of the creek. Soon he feels the detrimental effects of the polluted water to his bowels. He runs to a place behind the rocks, and in several fits all his bowels are turned empty. Then Cándido collapses in the sand "like a puppet with the strings cut" (p. 54). At that moment two juveniles (Jack Jr. and his pal) approach the shelter, devastate it and leave a graffiti behind on the rocks: "BEANERS DIE".

Meanwhile América is waiting at the labor exchange. After some time a big drunk American woman sits down next to her. América realizes with a shock that even in the land of plenty some of its citizens have to earn their living in this degrading way. At noon, when the labor exchange is closed, América walks aimlessly around, when she suddenly feels the hard stares of her Mexican countrymen. She is then reminded of the ruthless and aggressive behavior of the Mexicans when she crossed the border together with Cándido.

They had been attacked and one man tried to rape her. She quickly leaves the labor exchange and hurries to their shelter to find it completely devastated.

Chapter 5
Delaney and Kyra – their work

On his way home from the meeting Delaney has a frightening experience. A bulky American car turns into the dark street – there is no street lighting in Arroyo Blanco – and drives very slowly alongside him. The heavy thumping rhythm of rap music comes out of the car whose rolled-up windows are smoked so that Delaney cannot see inside. Delaney starts to walk faster, but the car keeps pace with him. Finally it accelerates, turns round at the end of the dead-end street and slowly rolls back down the block creeping past Delaney. Then it disappears. Safely at home, Delaney for the first time begins to think that perhaps the gate is not such a bad idea after all.
Kyra is waiting for him in bed reading erotic literature. For Kyra, sex is "a release from sorrow, tension, worry" (p. 65). With the disappearance of her beloved dog this day has been full of unusual emotional distress so that she now is especially eager and passionate. Lovemaking ends abruptly when Kyra thinks of her dog and Delaney has to confess that the dog is dead and that the only remains, the dog's paw, is in the freezer. In a frenzy Kyra verifies his statement suffering a terrible shock. She cannot sleep half the night, and only after the greatest efforts is she ready to keep her appointments the following day.
First she shows an unpleasant and overcritical couple around a once very impressive house, then she can welcome only six people at an open-house party in a newly listed house. For the rest of the afternoon she busies herself in the realtor's office fighting against her vicious headache. As usual, on her way home she checks and closes up five houses for the night. Kyra loves that ritual even if it means an extra hour of work. One of the houses, a huge place in the style of an English manor house, attracts her so much that she always spends a lot of time there, dreaming of owning it herself one day.
When Kyra has left that morning, Delaney buries the dog's paw and turns to work on his latest essay for his column called "Pilgrim at Topanga Creek". This time Delaney reports on his observations, thoughts and feelings when he camps out in the open nature of the Santa Monica Mountains. He celebrates the wonders of nature and feels elated to be able to be "part of the whole grand scheme of things, drinking from the same fount as the red-tailed hawk, the mule deer, the centipede and the scorpion too" (p. 78). In stark contrast to his latest experience of the coyote as a predator, he concludes his article with a song of praise for the coyote:

> "[...] this is what I've been waiting for all along: the coyote chorus. The song of the survivor, the Trickster, the four-legged wonder who can find water where there is none and eat hearty among the rocks and the waste places. [...] I lie back and listen, as on another night I might listen to Mozart or Mendelssohn, lulled by the impassioned beauty of it. The waterfall trickles. The coyotes sing. I have a handful of raisins and a blanket: what more could I want? All the world knows I am content." (p. 79)

Chapter 6
Cándido and América – their work

After a bitter quarrel in which Cándido even slaps América hard in the face América again goes up to the labor exchange to try her luck on "the fifth weary day in a row" (p. 80). In spite of her resistance a Mexican she has seen waiting at the labor exchange the last two mornings, forces his company on her. In a menacing manner he grabs her ankle and questions her faithfulness as a wife. Later a huge fat American drives up to the exchange and, to América's surprise, hires her. After the protest of the drunk American woman he picks up both and drives to his home in Arroyo Blanco. Here they have to clean blackened Buddha figurines with a corrosive. Then they stick glossy labels reading JIM SHIRLEY IMPORTS on them. In spite of the acid fumes and of her soon aching hands América works relentlessly without pause till in the evening. Then the American appears again and orders them to go to his car. América sits in the back closely watching the beautiful gardens and houses in this residential area. She notices that at the end of the residential road they drive through a **newly erected gate** which must have been built on this same day. She remembers that in the morning half a dozen of **her own people**, maybe also a Mexican from the labor exchange, were working there. Their American employer, Jim Shirley, drives the drunk lady home first; then he orders América to sit in the front seat beside him. On their way to the labor exchange the fat man lays his hand "casually across her thigh [...] she wanted to fling it away from her, hack it off with a machete and bury it in some bruja's yard, but she didn't" (p. 97).
During this long day Cándido is building a new shelter some way further up the creek. He constructs a new hearth and collects firewood hoping America would bring home some food, "some *tortillas* or a piece of meat and something to cook down into a stew, some vegetables and rice or a couple of potatoes ..." (p. 86 f.). Exhausted he takes a little nap. After a while he wakes up realizing with a jolt that América might not find the new shelter. He hurries to the place of the old camp to see that América is not there. So despite his pains he starts walking up the hill to meet América there at the end of the trail.
When he is halfway up, the same Mexican who molested América in the

morning comes downhill looking for a place to camp. Cándido evades the man's insistent inquiries about this canyon and finally finds a way to make the man feel uneasy so that this unpleasant figure wearing a baseball cap turned backwards on his head suddenly disappears down the trail. Cándido hurries on up to the parking lot and peers into the stores near the labor exchange hoping to see América. Feeling very faint from his long lack of food he unintentionally walks into a huge fat man with an Elvis-like hairdo in the parking lot of the shopping plaza. This man explodes with great verbal aggressiveness and shoves him away with a violent thrust of the arms. Cándido excuses himself and backs away with all the Americans there watching him.

Chapter 7
Delaney and his second meeting with Cándido

While cooking dinner one evening Delaney notices that there is no pasta for the marinara sauce he has already prepared. He takes his son Jordan and swiftly drives down to the supermarket. He rushes through the aisles of the market picking up the pasta and a few more things. As chance will have it, Delaney runs into Jack Jardine Sr. whom he has not seen since the meeting ten days ago. Although he is in a great hurry, he cannot help entering into a lengthy discussion with Jack Sr. about the gate, the Tortilla Curtain, illegal immigration and the U.S.A. as a country of immigrants. On the urging of the impatient Jack they leave the supermarket to become witnesses of an altercation going on in the parking lot. A Mexican is attacked by a big American with an Elvis-like hairdo and pushed onto the rear of Delaney's car. To his horror Delaney recognizes the Mexican he injured two weeks ago. "The man stood there a long moment, squinting into Delaney's eyes, the rag of a sling hanging from his arm, his face sunk in its helmet of bruises, and then he turned away and limped across the lot" (p. 105).

Meanwhile Kyra shows a couple as potential buyers around her favorite house, the Da Ros place. In contrast to her skillful verbosity with which she usually conducts her business she is strangely reserved today. She feels that these people do not deserve such a wonderful home. "The more time she spent in it, cushioned from the hot, dry, hard-driving world, the more she began to feel it was hers" (p. 107). The Greuterts do want a house "out of the way" (p. 107), outside crowded Los Angeles, a house like this one, and they tour it for nearly two and a half hours, but in the end decide not to take it.
This evening's dinner is a gloomy affair for the Mossbachers. The prepared meal is of course ruined by Delaney's neglect, Kyra is lost in her dreams, Jordan is not hungry, and the two remaining pets seem to mourn for their deceased companion.

The following morning Delaney is sitting at his keyboard trying to work out some new ideas for his "Pilgrim" column. He fails, however, as he is haunted by the image of the badly injured Mexican, "his Mexican" (p. 109). He is still so confused about the whole affair that he both feels guilty as a perpetrator and, at the same time, persecuted like a victim. To find relief for his troubled mind he starts on his planned afternoon hike into the canyon early. He parks his car just behind the machines of a road-working crew and climbs down to the streambed. To his horror he perceives the debris of a wild camp on the opposite bank of the creek. He suppresses his first impulse to clean up the mess on the spot. He decides to continue his hike and report on his discovery at the Sheriff's Department in the evening. Farther up the creek, where the canyon becomes narrow, Delaney's pleasure walk is utterly disturbed. He hears Spanish-speaking voices and is soon confronted with a Mexican and his Indian companion.

> "Delaney looked from the first man to his companion and back again. He wasn't alarmed, not exactly – he was too angry for that. All he could think of was the sheriff and getting these people and their garbage heap out of here, of hustling them right back to wherever they'd come from, slums, *favelas, barrios*, whatever they called them. They didn't belong here, that was for sure." (p. 116f.)

With more anger rising in him Delaney ends his hike and walks back to where he parked his car half an hour ago. It was gone. He learns that the road workers have not towed it away and that they have not noticed anything. So Delaney is compelled to walk the three miles up on the canyon road to get to the nearest telephone outside the grocery. The police and the towing service of the town have no information for him about his car. He then phones Kyra and tells her about the theft of his car.

Chapter 8
América and her second encounter with José Navidad

After the humiliating incident in the parking lot Cándido hides behind a shrub still hoping to meet América coming back here. He feels haunted by all kinds of devils: first this huge bully with the Elvis hair, then the red-haired car driver who ran him down on the canyon road, and – to top the list – the carrot-top youngster who devastated their camp. Cándido asks himself why he deserves such a kind of persecution. "Even Job would have broken down under an assault like this" (p. 121).
Finally América comes along in Jim Shirley's big Mercedes. She goes straight into the supermarket. Here she is joined by Cándido, and in great happiness they buy some food from América's first earned dollars. They walk down to their new camp, prepare dinner and enjoy for once the luxury of proper food.

The following morning both Cándido and América walk up to the labor exchange. Whereas Cándido is not selected by the patrons, América is again picked up by Jim Shirley to go on with cleaning his Buddhas. Today the acid corrosive has stronger effects on her hands and eyes. Only after long reflection does she screw up her courage to make herself heard in the huge empty house and ask for gloves. She works very hard the whole day to demonstrate her willingness and efficiency, but Jim Shirley with zero reaction takes no notice whatsoever. At six he drives her back to the parking lot, gives her twenty-five dollars, but otherwise ignores her presence.
América waits for Cándido to appear, but he does not. After quite some time she loses patience and longs for that little protection their make-shift shelter gives them. She walks down the trail, but there she is expected and attacked by two men, one tall man with a baseball cap worn reversed and a smaller, darker man: José Navidad and his Indian companion. She immediately turns round to run away from them. But they soon catch her and rape her.

Part Two: El Tenksgeevee

Chapter 1
Delaney and Kyra – on the defensive

Delaney is full of indignation at the indifference with which people react to the theft of his car. The Acura car dealer, Kenny Grisson, can hardly conceal how pleased he is, since he now can sell a brand-new car. To him car thefts are commonplace events in the L.A. area with its many immigrants. By contrast Delaney sees his well-ordered life under attack and his security shattered. The police treat the car lift as a negligable routine case and his friend Jack again just feels affirmed in his views on immigration.The Americans are "under siege here" (p. 146) in their own country.
With his brand-new look-alike Acura car Delaney drives to an Indian restaurant to meet Kyra there for lunch. To have his car parked he has to hand it over to a parking attendant, "[he] was Mexican, of course – Hispanic, Latino, whatever" – (p. 147), who drives the new car to a parking lot round the corner of the building. The new car has no personalized license plates (the old car had PILGRIM on them), but just a random sequence of letters and numbers which Delaney still does not know. At this moment he feels he is losing control over his life.
They take their lunch in a hurry as Kyra shortly has an appointment. On leaving the restaurant they notice that in a jeep parked nearby a dog is locked in and suffering from the great heat. Kyra is incensed at this thoughtless cruelty and tries to find the driver to call him to account. When she sees him, she furiously accuses him of cruelty to his dog. The stolid dog-owner is com-

pletely unimpressed and with deft curses for Kyra and Delaney just drives off leaving them behind trembling with anger and defeat.
To get away from the nastiness of people Delaney drives towards the ocean hills to seek refuge there for a few hours. Near a trail he parks his new car on a parking strip along the road. He takes his small satchel with the bottled water and sets out on the trail for an afternoon hike. "He didn't get far. He kept thinking about that new car [...]. Suddenly, without thinking, he sank into the brush no more than a hundred yards from the road" (p. 155). Torn between his desire to enjoy a good walk and his anxiety to be robbed of his car a second time he cannot make up his mind what to do. Although he knows that this is paranoic, he just sits down there in the brush watching his car which glitters in the sunlight through the stalks and branches.
On her way to her afternoon appointment Kyra notices that at the 7-Eleven parking lot on Ventura Boulevard the formerly small group of Mexicans waiting to be hired there for work has meanwhile become a big crowd of fifty or more. As she also does estate business in this area, she decides to counteract this new development, because it might scare away potential buyers. She turns into the parking lot and under the stares of the Mexicans she goes into the store to find out what people think about this bustling labor exchange. The two Asian shopkeepers are not willing to take side for anyone. On her way back to the car Kyra is approached by a young Mexican who does not step aside but doggedly asks her to hire him for work. She escapes into her car and drives off, by now convinced that "somebody had to do something about these people – they were ubiquitous, prolific as rabbits, and they where death for business" (p. 158).
Between two further appointments Kyra decides to drop in at home to see if Al Lopez and his men are building the fence the way she wants to have it. While inspecting the fence Kyra notices in one of Al Lopez' workers "the man with the limp and the graying mustache, his face bruised and swollen like a bad fruit. [...] This was the man, the very man – it had to be" (p. 161).
In the evening Kyra makes her usual round shutting up "her" houses for the night. At her favorite place, the Da Roses' mansion, she is annoyed and concerned at seeing a shopping cart in the ditch along the private road leading up to the house. She checks and shuts up the house with special care and caution. When she is about to leave, she notices two men beyond the lawn. Fearlessly she walks up to them and tells them to keep off private property. However, the tall man with a baseball cap worn reversed on his head is not impressed at all, but fixes his cruel eyes on Kyra with such a hate that she falters and becomes afraid. After some uneasy moments for Kyra the tall man exchanges a look of understanding with the smaller man indicating that they should leave Kyra and the place without doing any further harm.

Chapter 2
Cándido – hired and fired: a barbecue of discontent

The labor exchange has already been closed at half past twelve earlier that same day when Al Lopez hires the still waiting Cándido to replace one of his sick workers. Al Lopez is going to put up a high fence around a big house in one of the new developments and Cándido is only too glad to help him. Cándido does not resent the gate at the entrance and the fences around the development nor does he envy the ostentatious wealth of the residents of the gated city. Beyond any envy the only idea in his head is work, any work. So he is elated to do the jobs Al Lopez gives him, also the fence job at that rich man's house in Arroyo Blanco.

Cándido's thoughts wander back to the time when after the potato harvest in Idaho he went south to California and ended up here in L.A. County for the first time. He had a very narrow escape from L.A. *Migra*, the immigration police who had made a sweep of the entire area. He had managed to break free, fled across the highway and hid in the Topanga Canyon. His memory of this incident is still painful to him, as one of his companions wanted to do likewise and was killed in the highway traffic.

Having finally found work, earning money for him and América arouses feelings of relief and satisfaction in Cándido. In high spirits and fifty dollars richer he ends his first workday very late and hurries to América in the canyon. Here he finds an utterly bewildered woman who shrinks back from his touch. He learns that José Navidad and the Indian attacked her and stole their money. América sternly denies having been raped, but Cándido is not really convinced of this.

He does not allow her to to take up a day-labor job any more, and so América spends all the following days in their camp leading a very miserable and troubled life. She does not feel well, there seem to be injuries caused by the rape, and above all, being only seventeen years old, she feels left alone and helpless in her proceeding pregnancy. She knows that she needs assistance and longs to be back with her mother.

After three weeks of steady employment and good money from Al Lopez, Cándido is fired because the worker he has replaced for the time of his absence is well again. Moreover, this man has the advantage of the green card. In great frustration Cándido comes home and willingly gets drunk in the course of a crude barbecue dinner. He rages around and, still suspicious of what José Navidad might have done to América, Cándido threatens and beats her.

> "But as he lay there watching the sparks climb into the sky, the wine infesting his veins, he knew how it was going to be, how it had to be, knew he would follow her into that hut and slap his own pain out of her, and that was so sick and so bad he wanted nothing more in that moment than to die" (p. 182).

Chapter 3:
Delaney and Kyra: a barbecue of content ending in another kind of cruelty

Life is running smoothly again for Delaney and his family. They enjoy a fine barbecue at the pool on a sunny Sunday evening in mid-August. At dinner the conversation turns to the 7-Eleven labor exchange on Ventura Boulevard. Kyra admits that the area there has been "cleaned up" on her initiative, whereupon Delaney lapses into an interior struggle of feelings. On the one hand this means the violation of basic "inalienable" rights, but on the other hand he feels that the situation is rapidly worsening. He recollects the informal meeting of neighbors two nights before at Dominick Flod's place. Here the hardliners gathered to launch the campaign for greater security: they were planning to have the labor exchange at the Topanga post office "cleaned up" and, most importantly, they wanted to build a seven-foot wall around their development to prevent any intrusion. Without the wall the newly erected gate was useless, they maintained. Delaney, who is still having very mixed and conflicting thoughts about the wall, resolves just to forget about it and to enjoy the pleasant summer evening and their refined barbecue in good feeling with Kyra.

Suddenly first Kyra and then Delaney see a coyote on their lawn inside the fence stalking and grabbing the little terrier. Despite their cries of horror the coyote keeps his prey, climbs over the new high fence in no time and disappears into the hillside brush.

Chapter 4
Cándido – the closure of the labor exchange

Cándido is employed for five days in a row clearing the brush in a canyon to make room for the extension of a new development. It is hard work, badly paid and on top of it he is swindled, for he does not get the money for the fifth day. On the following days he goes to the labor exchange in vain. One morning he finds it "closed" on his arrival. The man who donated the place for this service has withdrawn his permission and the pillars and the shelter have already been removed. "Posts had been driven into the ground at each of the two entrances, and they were linked by chains thick enough to anchor a boat. The signs were nailed to the posts. PRIVATE, they screamed in blazing red letters, ALL PERSONS WARNED AGAINST TRESPASS" (p. 198). This is a bad blow for Cándido; he feels great injustice as he is denied the human right of work by super-rich Americans. Confused he does the rounds of the lot near the post office. Suddenly his eyes are attracted by a briefcase in a **Lexus** car whose windows are rolled down. He feels strongly tempted to steal the briefcase which he imagines to be full of money. This would solve all his immediate troubles: an apartment for his pregnant wife and his soon to be born "son". But before he has resolved his inner struggle of take it or leave it, a lady, who in all details given much resembles Kyra (we have learned earlier that she drives a Lexus; see p. 31), comes back and presses a few coins into Cándido's hand as if he was a beggar.

América welcomes the news of the closure of the labor exchange, as this might mean the escape from the hated camp, the place of her greatest humiliation and constant frustration. She persuades Cándido to give it a try and walk to San Fernando Valley to find an apartment there and, if possible, work. The next day they leave their camp for the ten-mile walk. On their arrival in San Fernando Valley América is delighted to see the fashionable shops which make her forget the extreme strain of the long walk. They walk on to Canoga Park where América is surprised to find a "little Mexico". They have a Mexican dinner in a Mexican place before they walk up and down the streets for hours to find a place to stay for the night. In the evening they rest exhausted on a low wall in front of the Canoga Park post office, when a Mexican-American approaches them and offers them a cheap apartment in the vicinity. After some consideration Cándido accompanies the stranger to have a look at the apartment leaving América behind in the street.

Chapter 5
The PILGRIM'S appraisal of the coyote

In his new contribution for the naturalist magazine Delaney presents his enlightened view on the coyote in North America. To his mind the conflict between the urban sprawl into formerly coyote country and the backlash of the coyote can only be solved if man accepts the intrusion of the animal as a fact and behaves accordingly.

Chapter 6
Delaney and Kyra: losing ground

The encounter with the two men at the Da Ros place has shattered Kyra's fearlessness and self-assertion. Moreover, she no longer enjoys her daily visits to her once favorite dream house, she even considers the house to be a burden and fears it might become a failure as an estate object. Now she enters the house with mixed feelings and makes her usual round checking everything. As a precaution she has an arrangement with the estate agent's secretary according to which Darlene will phone the police if Kyra does not report back after 15 minutes that she is about to leave. Today everything seems to be in order till she walks round the back of the house. There her eyes are hit by a six-foot-high spray-paint inscription across the side of the house reading: PINCHE PUTA ("damned whore").

On her way to the Da Ros place Kyra remembered her evening appointment with two women of their neighborhood to discuss their assistance in Jack Jardine`s campaign for the "wall". She was persuaded by him to join the team. Jack cleverly explained to her that in this way no coyote would ever try to get in. Kyra learned the phrase "They do not stalk and hunt what they cannot see" – and therefore was in Jack`s boat.
So one evening she sets out on the difficult task to persuade Delaney, too. Delaney cannot believe that Kyra supports the plans for the wall. To him the sheer idea is absurd whereas she welcomes that wall to satisfy her wish for security, especially against coyotes. Their disagreement escalates into a bitter argument with shouts and insults. Delaney forbids Kyra to join the wall committee, Kyra in defiance just turns away from him and buries herself in work. The quarrell ends in a serious estrangement between husband and wife.

After a paddleball (squash) workout at the community center Delaney happens to overhear the half-joking half-serious racist slurs of Jack Jr. and one of his friends. It comes down on Delaney like a revelation that this community is poisonous and that also his stepson Jordan will be infected by it. "The whole place was poisonous, the whole state. He wished he'd stayed in New York" (p. 225). On his way back home he is addressed by two of the activists opposing the wall. In his present mood he is only too eager to agree with their views, but when he is requested to actively help their cause he shrinks back. He realizes that no matter what his convictions are his recent experiences, the conflict with his wife and his friendship with Jack Jardine compel him to refrain from taking part in the anti-wall campaign. With a lame excuse he hurries home. When he turns into his street, he notices a Mexican with a shoulder bag slung over his arm in the front garden of the Cherrystones' house. Walking up to him to call him to account he recognizes him as the man with the baseball cap turned backwards (José Navidad). Steamed up he commands the supposed trespasser to leave the area. He is in such a state that he has not noticed the Mexican's job: he is distributing fliers to all the houses in the street.

> "Delaney took a step back, so devastated he couldn't speak – what was happening to him, what was he becoming? – and the man shoved the flier into his hand and stalked away across the lawn. He watched, stupefied, as the Mexican headed up the street, carrying his shoulders with rage and indignation, watched as he strode up to Delaney's own house and inserted a flier in the slit between the screen door and the white wooden doorframe. Then, finally, Delaney looked down at the sheet of paper in his hand. A SPECIAL MESSAGE FROM THE PRESIDENT OF THE ARROYO BLANCO ESTATES PROPERTY OWNERS' ASSOCIATION […]. 'I urge all of you to attend Wednesday's meeting on an issue vital to the security and well-being of us all …'" (p. 229).

Chapter 7
Cándido and América – hitting rock bottom

América has to wait almost till midnight before Cándido comes back to the Canoga Park post office. He has to wake up América who, exhausted from the day, has fallen asleep on a wall in front of the building. Upon his touch she starts up seeing that Cándido is in a terrible state. There is blood all over his face, his clothes are torn and he has desperate news for her: "They got everything" (p. 234). The Mexican had led him to a dark alley where he was brutally attacked and robbed of all their money. América's greatest wish and only dream for a roof over her head if only for one night turns into a nightmare.

> "There would be no bed, no shower, no dinner even. And in he future: no apartment, no shops, no restaurants, no toys and blankets and diapers for her baby. Her mind raced ahead and back again, and then she thought of the woods, of the canyon, of that shitpile of sticks, and she wanted to die" (p. 234f.).

Cándido leads her to a gas station where they use the toilet to wash that blood away from Cándido`s face. After that Cándido decides to walk back. Turning into the canyon road they approach a restaurant. To the horror and disgust of América Cándido climbs into the big leftover bin. When he backs out of it, his arms are spilling over with little cardboard boxes filled with cooking grease gone cold. He passes one box to América saying, "'Eat, *mi vida*,' [...]. 'You're going to need it to keep up your strength'" (p. 239).

Chapter 8
Delaney and Kyra – Cándido and América: Thanksgiving Day

(Note that this chapter incorporates both strands of the story.)

During his sacrosanct writing hours in the morning Delaney, who is reflecting on the effects of the hot, dry California fall, is disturbed by a Mexican workcrew who need access through his garden to build the wall behind his house. After 90 percent of the wall has already been built, this is the last link of the fortification which robs Delaney of his view and cuts down his spontaneity to go for a stroll. Whereas he had not taken part in any action on either side, had not even attended the decisive community meeting, Kyra's great efforts were vital for the success of the wall mission. In the end the result of the vote was 127 to 87 in favor of the wall. With the workers in his garden Delaney cannot concentrate on his writing any longer. All he can do is watch the wall go up walling him in and burying him alive (p. 244).

After the graffiti incident Delaney has got used to accompanying Kyra in the evening to the Da Ros place. Their relationship is still strained by the wall business, but they are again on speaking terms. As a gesture of good will and understanding Kyra presents him with a ladder which allows him to scale the wall whenever he wants to. On their way back from the Da Ros place they stop at a supermarket to buy a last few things for the feast they are planning for Thanksgiving. While they are together selecting the many delicatessen articles, Delaney's grudge against Kyra softens. Watching her movements he longingly feels attracted by her, and suddenly has his hands on her hips and gives her a kiss. To his surprise she kisses him back. And he is surprised once more when Kyra accepts the market's offer of a free turkey, though they have already got one at home.

Cándido and América again live in the canyon. Cándido does not mind the hot fall with the sandstorms, if only it stays dry and sunny for two more months. What he fears is the following rainy season, as this will be the time when their baby is expected to be born. Lately Cándido is much troubled by América's state of mind. Full of apathy she is drawn within herself unwilling to do anything. "She wouldn't talk to him. She refused to cook. She stopped washing her hair and her body and within the week she stank like one of the homeless, like a wild thing, like a corpse" (p. 250). In spite of the closure of the labor exchange Cándido finds work with an eccentric Mexican-American constructor, Señor Willis, who treats and pays him very well. "Señor Willis proved to be a surprise [...], the best surprise Cándido had had since he left Tepoztlán" (p. 251). However, on the morning of Thanksgiving Day he is told by Señor Willis that there will be no work that day. He goes up to the supermarket to buy two bottles of beer as a social holiday treat for himself and a few things which he hopes might cheer up América. Two male customers at the checkout cannot decide about what to do with the store's complimentary turkey. They finally leave it to Cándido who cannot believe his luck. Even América has to smile when Cándido, the big frozen bird in his arms, comes back and plays the fool for her. And to his surprise América starts to prepare the turkey for the barbecue which arouses a feeling of great happiness in Cándido. "He was happy, as happy as he'd ever been" (p. 257). But this happiness lasts only a few moments, because exactly then "the wind plucked the fire out of its bed of coals and with a roar as loud as all the furnaces of hell set it dancing in the treetops" (p. 257). In his joy he has not been careful enough with the fire; it flares up high and gets out of control.

Part Three: Socorro

Chapter 1
Delaney and Kyra – the Thanksgiving cocktail party

On smelling the roasting turkey Delaney's heart is seized by the spirit of Thanksgiving, and he nostalgically remembers the fine wintry atmosphere of Thanksgiving back home in New England. Delaney and Kyra are going to have a traditional Thanksgiving dinner in the evening together with their neighbors, the Cherrystones and the Jardines, and Kyra's mother Kit Menaker who has come over from San Francisco. In the afternoon, however, they go over to Dominick Flood's cocktail party which is celebrated in grand style: there are about a hundred guests from Arroyo Blanco and from outside, there are heaps of exquisite food, a string quartet tries to entertain the noisy crowd, and everybody seems to be enjoying themselves except Delaney who feels a bit out of place and whose mind is troubled about how his own dinner party will run. Kyra thoroughly enjoys the party. She feels intrigued by their somewhat mysterious host Dom Flood with his electronic shackle around his ankle. Even Kyra's mother – fifty-five years old, divorced – gets into full swing and immediately falls for this temporary bachelor who has been left by his wife. Kit never budges from Dom Flod's side trying to turn his head. Delaney's mood does not improve. He becomes even more pensive when Kyra and Jack make use of the relaxed atmosphere to challenge him on his attitude towards the wall and his views on the intruding coyotes.

Suddenly at about four in the afternoon there is a fire alarm. Helicopters appear in the sky and smoke rises up from the canyon. Not yet knowing if this is going to be one of the many small brushfires common to this area or if it turns out to be a fatal blast Delaney and Kyra leave the party immediately to look after Jordan. At home they turn on the TV to see that in the lower canyon there rages an intense and extensive fire. Kyra orders her family to load the car. All look at Delaney as the authority to decide on the question of leaving. Everbody understands when he says: "'We better shut off the turkey' [...]. 'Just in case.'"(p. 271)

Chapter 2
Cándido and América: escaping from the fire

Seeing Cándido coming back with that huge bird and trying to cheer her up, América (*her perspective*) decides to give up her grudge against him. Her spirits brighten, the leaves and the sky seem to regain their colors to her, and she gets up from the ground and holds Cándido. She is so happy to feel alive again that she does not hear the increasing roar of the raging fire around the camp.

Cándido (*his perspective*) at once realizes the great danger of a fire in the canyon. He clearly sees that their only chance to save their lives is to climb up the rock wall at the end of their camp and follow up the creek to the top of the mountain. In a frenzy Cándido makes América crawl up the overhanging rock in shoving her heavy body up the wall. Up there he makes her hurry on up the streambed. "He urged her on. Shoved and shouted and half-carried her" (p. 275). At a turning of the creek the gorge widens and reveals a rubbish dump consisting of all kinds of junk which has been dumped from the road down into the canyon. This is their way out. "América, sweating, bleeding, tears of rage and fear and frustration in her eyes, began to climb up over the hood of an accordioned car, her belly swinging out and away from her like an untethered balloon" (p. 276).

At the top they find the canyon road in a bustle of firefighters and police. To stay undetected they quickly rush further up the road and hide for a moment behind the building of the Chinese store. Hot and exhausted they gulp water from a hose there, wet their faces and soak their clothes. Then they walk up the brush towards the western rim of the canyon. Halfway up América sinks down under the onset of the beginning labor-pains. Cándido reassures her and swiftly walks up to find one of the now deserted houses of a residential area. He hits upon a garden shed along a white stucco wall, lights a kerosene lamp and then guides América to the shed. "She couldn't believe she was having her baby in a place like this, with the whole world on fire and nobody to help her, no midwife, no doctor, not even a *curandera*" (p. 282). She can hardly bear the terrible pains coming regularly at short intervals. Lying helplessly in the shed América is joined by a pretty Siamese cat coming right up to her. "She held out her hand, and then clenched her fist with the pain of a contraction, and the cat stayed with her. '*Gatita*,'she whispered to the arching back and the blue luminous eyes, 'you're the one. You're the saint. You. You will be my midwife'" (p. 283).

Chapter 3
Delaney and Kyra – watching the fire

The residents of the Arroyo Blanco development are evacuated and most of them first hold out in their heavily loaded cars at the top of Topanga Canyon. The frightened Kyra cannot stand hearing Delaney's sarcastic remark about the loss of the turkey and resentfully turns away from him. To calm down Delaney accepts Jack Cherrystone`s offer of a drink, takes the whisky bottle and downs a solid gulp of Scotch. He can hardly believe his eyes when he instantly sees two men coming up the canyon road and recognizes in one of them José Navidad and his companion. Jack and Delaney walk up to the roadblock, where a Hispanic-looking patrolman is already questioning the two men. In great excitement Delaney informs him about having seen the two men "'camping right down there where the fire started'" (p. 287). When this leaves the patrolmen unimpressed, Jack Cherrystone, the movie actor with the resounding and commanding voice, has his scene. Audible to a large gathering crowd he confirms Delaney's accusation and emphatically demands decisive police action against the alleged arsonists. With calm determination and swift action another policeman, who has joined his colleague, has the two men on the ground in a second. They are handcuffed and hauled to their feet right in front of Delaney. When the second policeman pulls at José's arm to march him off, José answers Delaney's victorious look with spitting him into the face. Delaney loses control and ferociously attacks the handcuffed Mexican. The situation threatens to escalate, as there is a violent outburst of aggressiveness from the crowd.

At midnight the fire is still raging so that Delaney and Kyra decide to stay for the rest of the night at the Holiday Inn at Woodland Hills. Actually the fire does not do much harm to Arroyo Blanco. At the very last moment the hot Santa Ana winds change and make way for the moist ocean air to settle over the scourged area. The fire has burned to within five hundred yards of Arroyo Blanco, before it swerves west and finally dies down. By ten in the morning everybody can return to their Arroyo Blanco homes. There Delaney and Kyra find everything untouched by the fire and the heat blast, but to the great sorrow of Jordan their Siamese cat, Dame Edith, is missing. Kyra hears unconfirmed reports that the Da Ros place has been completely destroyed by the fire. Kyra's mother, who is utterly shaken by the events anyway, suffers a crushing blow of shame and hurt when she detects Dom Flood`s electronic shackle in her purse. Dom has apparently misused their intimacy to get rid of the device by smuggling it into Kit's purse.

Chapter 4
Cándido and América: the birth of Socorro

While the fire is raging up to their small shed, América gives birth to their baby on Thanksgiving night. Cándido acts as midwife as best as he can and the baby is born alive and well. He is overjoyed assuming that the baby can only be a boy. But nevertheless, after some moments of irritation, he also welcomes his new-born daughter with fatherly pride. América has stood the delivery well. In a dreamy voice and great contentment she announces that she is going to call the girl Socorro. She goes to sleep with the baby lying in her arm and the cat Dame Edith nestling in the bend of her leg.
After the delivery Cándido is out watching the fire approach and then recedes from the roof of the shed. He has realized by now that he knows the

residential area behind the wall from his job with Al Lopez. Assuming that the houses will be deserted for a few more hours he decides to take the opportunity of procuring some food and the things he needs to build a new shelter. In a frenzy of activities he climbs several times back and forth over the wall hauling the things to a more distant place where in great hurry he builds a new hut. Then, with patience but great determination, he forces the distraught and confused América to move over to their new shelter. In spite of the returning residents Cándido decides to go for a last haul to procure a large sheet of plastic for the roof to the hut. In one of the gardens he has a very narrow escape from the approaching residents and their dog, but he manages to slip through a gap into the neigboring garden which he recognizes to be the place where he helped to erect the fence. Here he notices a ladder (Delaney's) leaning against the wall, and in no time he is on the other side and out of sight. Having put the plastic sheet on the hut he falls into a deep sleep, utterly exhausted. He is awakened again by the intensive smell of fruit. He finds out that in the meantime América has sucked heaps of fruit to quench her thirst. He knows that his wife needs milk and meat instead to recover and to nurse the baby. While he is figuring out how he might get meat for a stew the Siamese cat which has followed them appears outside the hut. Cándido lures it to come to him.

Chapter 5
Kyra – assessing the damage; Delaney – on the prowl

As soon as the roads are open to public traffic again, Kyra drives through a desertlike area to the Da Ros place. She is shattered about the devastation and the loss of both her house and her dream. Full of anger her thoughts turn to the two Mexicans and supposed culprits. With utter disbelief she has received the news that the police have let them go for lack of evidence. She feels that this means giving the hordes of illegals a free hand in ruining the country and her business.

Late on Sunday afternoon Delaney and Kyra go out for a stroll to get relief from the tension of the past days. Jack Jardine, who happens to pass by with his car, stops and asks them to accompany him to the entrance gate. There, the outside wall is defaced with undecipherable graffiti on both sides of the gate. It is different from the one meant for Kyra at the Da Ros place, but Kyra is sure that she recognizes the Mexican style of the many graffiti you can see "all over the Valley – it's like their own code" (p. 316) to mark their territory.

In early December Delaney constructs a device by which people approaching the wall are photographed by secret cameras hidden left and right of the gate. One morning he finds both cameras have been triggered, although the wall is still unmarked. Delaney rushes to Jack Cherrystone's darkroom to develop the films. The face on the photo is Mexican, but it is not the one he expected, it does not belong to the man with the baseball cap turned backwards who spat at him. To his great surprise it turns out to be the face of "**his**" Mexican: Cándido.

Chapter 6
América – the mother; Cándido – the victim of a man hunt

On the one hand Cándido regards himself to be a total failure who has made a mess of his life, but on the other hand he still feels some pride in having been able to provide América with the basic needs of life: food and shelter. América is happy with her baby and the successful birth has strenghtened her self-confidence She appreciates Cándido's ceaseless toil and understanding support, but in spite of this she is convinced that Cándido will never be able to provide her and the baby with a decent standard of living. She believes that everything he does turns out wrong: "This wasn't just bad luck, this was an ongoing catastrophe, and how long could they survive that?" (p. 324). América regards it as her duty to have Socorro baptized, in the first place to have her registered as proof of her existence and her American citizenship, but then also to adhere to the traditions of her Christian faith. The question of how and where to get this done is left unsettled. With great apprehension she one day notices that the baby on her arm is invariably staring past her and that the baby's eyes do not turn to follow her moving hand. They just stare into empty space.

As their savings have been destroyed in the fire, Cándido is forced to hang around the post office and other places in the village in the hope of being hired. However, the fire has produced a xenophobic climate in the community. Dispirited he gives up his endeavors for the day and starts walking on the canyon road. His reflections on how to get some food are abruptly interrupted when a car swerves right in front of him. The door of it swings open, and to his exasperation Cándido recognizes the man who ran him down almost at the same spot some months ago and who now shouts at him fiercely.

Chapter 7
Delaney – stalking his enemy

Driving up the canyon road with his car full of plants and fertilizer Delaney's view is arrested by a pedestrian on the road he suspects he knows well. To identify him he swerves his car onto the shoulder without paying any attention to the cars following him. He does not even care that the rear end of his car partly blocks the road. His interest is totally absorbed by the fact that he has finally met "his" Mexican. Delaney shouts to him to stay where he is and dials 911 to have him arrested. While Delaney is talking to the police, Cándido uses the opportunity to cross the road and run away regardless of

the heavy traffic. A woman driver trying to avoid hitting him skids into the guardrail and then bounces into the back end of Delaney's car. The policeman who arrives after twenty minutes questions the woman and Delaney separately. He takes no notice of Delaney's argument of the suicidal Mexican and coldly informs him that he alone is to blame for the accident: "'Your vehicle was obstructing the road'" (p. 334). When the tow truck arrives to load his car, Delaney tells the driver that he is going to walk the short distance home.
Meanwhile Kyra is on her way to pick up Jordan at his friend's house. She does not know exactly where this is and so she waits for quite some time near the presumed address. In one of the gardens there is a sign saying FOR SALE BY OWNER. She cannot resist checking this out and starts up the drive. Half a mile in the park-like garden she catches sight of a marvellous house putting the Da Ros place into the shade by far. She knows how to proceed in such a case and presses the bell. Without hesitation she is invited by the owners to have a look at the house.

Delaney, an expert on tracing animal footprints, has no problem following the Mexican's track up the hill. It clearly leads to Arroyo Blanco, but then the traces are dissolved by the heavy rain. In the rain and darkness Delaney checks on the gate and notices that the wall has again been defaced by new graffiti. Now with the knowledge that "his" Mexican must be camping out somewhere in the vicinity he becomes increasingly sure that it was "his" Mexican who had stolen the things in the neighborhood on the night of the fire, that it is him who defaces the wall and that it was him who started the fire. In hectic activity Delaney checks his cameras to find out that only one has flashed. The other one has been damaged by force. In great excitement he hurries home, where he does not find Kyra and Jordan. He goes out to the garage and takes the gun which he bought about six months ago. In spite of the late night he goes over to the Cherrystones' house to have the film developed. As he knows that the Cherrystones are absent, he lets himself in with the key hidden under a potted plant in the garden. He works feverishly to develop the film, and to his utmost amazement the photo does not show the face of "his" Mexican but the figure of Jack Jardine Jr. and an accomplice caught in the act of spraying graffiti onto the wall. After the first shock Delaney methodically cleans everything up, crumples the negatives and the contact sheet into a ball and buries it deep in the trash.
This turn of events does not prevent Delaney from hunting down his main enemy: "his" Mexican, the trespasser and canyon arsonist. In the dark, rainy night he climbs over the wall with the gun in his pocket and makes his way through the heavy mud of the burned-out slopes. He has stalked a hundred different animals a hundred times here in this area; so he is sure that he will close in on this creature, too.

> "All that mattered was this, was finding him, rooting him out of his burrow and counting his teeth and his toes and the hairs on his head and noting it all down for the record. [...] There was no escaping him. And then, just as he knew he would, he caught the first faint reductive whiff of it: woodsmoke. Delaney touched the gun [...], and let his nose guide him" (p. 347).

Chapter 8
Delaney, Cándido and América: extending and grasping hands

(Note the alternating perspectives.)

Cándido is still shaken by the new encounter with his tormentor. To his mind the red-haired devil was again trying to run him over and kill him, though Cándido cannot imagine the reason. He is also unable to imagine that the American knows about the cause of the fire. After his supper of a heart-warming soup and some tortillas, Cándido's tenseness softens. Then América musters up all her courage to tell him that Socorro is blind and that this defect has been caused by José Navidad raping her. To Cándido this is the worst blow he has ever received in his life. But before he can react, something hits the outside of the hut and in the next moment the red-haired devil is standing in the doorway with a gun in his hand.

Delaney has found the campers' shack despite the darkness of the rainy night and the roar of water and rumbling mudslides. He jumps into the hut, when all of a sudden a huge mudslide heaves it up and sweeps Delaney and the three Mexicans together with their crushed shack down into the canyon.
To **Cándido's** mind three catastrophic events hit him at the same time: his daughter's blindness, this red-haired devil with a gun, and then the crushing mountain. Everything seems to tumble down on him at the same moment tending to annihilate him.

> "All he wanted was work, and this was his fate, this was his stinking *pinche* luck, a violated wife and a blind baby and a crazy white man with a gun, and even that wasn't enough to satisfy an insatiable God: no, they all had to drown like rats in the bargain" (p. 353).

Holding on to the pallet of their hut they are swept into a newly created stream. First Cándido, América and Socorro are still able to cling to each other on the dancing raft. Then their stream joins the canyon creek which has developed into a meter-high torrent inundating huge areas and flowing high over bridges and streets. Cándido is hurled from the raft. He fights with the water to stay on top and to grasp América's stretched-out hand. "Suddenly the water spat him up in his wife's arms" (p. 354), and in a miraculous way they get stranded and saved on top of the roof of the post office. Cándido feels América sobbing so hard that both their bodies are shaking. He is slow to recognize that their baby has gone. But then the amazing final event takes place:

“He was beyond cursing, beyond grieving, numbed right through to the core of him. All that, yes. But when he saw the white face surge up out of the black swirl of the current and the white hand grasping at the tiles, he reached down and took hold of it” (p. 355).

Handshake

IV Analysis and Interpretation

1. Structure

The narration of the novel follows the lives of two couples for about 7 months. They live in great proximity in the Topanga area, but in circumstances that could hardly be more different. On the side of Delaney and Kyra there is wealth, a prestigious house in a privileged housing area, two cars, satisfying work, friends, economic and social security, a refined lifestyle, and naturalist leisure walks, whereas there is poverty, insecurity, lack of work and food, no friends, going on foot by necessity, and a makeshift open air camp as shelter on the side of Cándido and América. The **haves**, satirated Americans who live their material American dream, are contrasted with the **have-nots**, illegal Mexican immigrants who struggle for survival and whose modest American dream of getting a job, of living in a decent apartment, and of leading a life in dignity and respect has turned into a nightmare.

The narrative material is arranged in a way in which – apart from a few variations – the 24 chapters alternately refer to either the American or the Mexican couple. Thus the lives of the two couples are continually **juxtaposed** and **contrasted** in a kind of **dual structure**. In addition, the contrast between the couples' lives is effectfully reinforced by **parallel situations**. Both families consist of a husband, his second wife and a child. But behind this parallel constellation fundamental differences become visible. Delaney's first wife had an abortion (p. 290), whereas Resurrección did not get pregnant in her marriage with Cándido. And regarding the "second wives" (América and Cándido are not formally married) América "is looking forward towards fulfilling herself as a mother" (P. Freese, p. 222), while Kyra rejects Delaney's one-year-long pleadings to have a baby. "She wouldn't hear of it – there was always another house to show, another listing, another deal to close" (p. 225).

This structural technique of parallelism and contrast can be observed throughout the novel. It is Boyle's "constitutive narrative strategy" to "gradually unveil the fundamental differences lurking behind seeming similarities" (P. Freese, p. 222). These differences are sometimes only too evident. Delaney, for example, reports in his "Pilgrim" column that he also camps out in nature, but just for his pleasure, for one night only and probably as a self-deluding justification of his coveted role as a "pilgrim" (Anne Dilliard, his model, camped out for a year to be close to nature; see p. 57).

There are many more examples: the Sunday barbecue in August with Delaney serving a vegetarian dinner with *Perrier* water at the pool is juxtaposed

and contrasted with Cándido roasting eight Italian sausages over the fire and eating them with tortillas before getting drunk on cheap wine (p. 179); both Delaney and Kyra and also Cándido do their Thanksgiving shopping at Gitello's supermarket on the morning of this day. But whereas Cándido after long hesitation buys only some modest food and as a special treat two bottles of Budweiser, Delaney and Kyra delve into the satisfying pleasure of shopping and loading their cart full of delicatessen items, although they have already spent two hundred and eighty dollars for their Thanksgiving Day party in a Woodland Hills superstore (p. 246). Moreover, while Kyra accepts the complimentary turkey offered to her at the checkout although she has already got one at home and really does not need a second one, Cándido is denied the turkey because of his low bill (p. 255).
Apart from these specific contrastive parallelisms we find that throughout the novel units of two chapters each are linked together by their common theme or situation. The headings selected and presented in our summary of the story (see Chapter III) try to illustrate this **structural parallelism**.

The novel shifts back and forth between the two story lines and the two worlds of the two couples in alternating fashion. Theoretically, each strand of the action can be seen independently. However, it is one of the main points of the novel to have the **Mexican and American spheres clash in a sequence of encounters** thus **interlinking and intertwining both worlds**. Sometimes these encounters between representatives of the two different spheres are uneventful, accidental contacts (for instance when Cándido helps Al Lopez building the fence in Delaney's garden and Kyra recognizes Cándido), but in most cases they happen under **dramatically heightened circumstances**: the tension and awkwardness following the road accident, the encounter between Delaney and Cándido in front of Gitello's supermarket, Cándido hesitating to pinch the briefcase from Kyra's car, Delaney blocking Cándido on the canyon road, Delaney jumping into the Mexican's hut with a gun in his hand and the final scene with Cándido saving Delaney's life.

Interlinking the two strands of action: American-Mexican encounters			
Part One			
Americans		**Mexicans**	**Encounters**
1	↔		Delaney crashes into Cándido (p. 3)
		2	
3			
	→	4	Jack Jr. devastates Cándido's and América's camp (p. 60)
5			
	↔	6	Jim Shirley hires América to work at his Arroyo Blanco house (p. 92)
7	→		Delaney's second encounter with Cándido (p. 104) Delaney comes across José Navidad (p. 116)
	←	8	Cándido's second encounter with Delaney (p. 121)
Part Two			
1	↔		Kyra meets Cándido on her own ground (p. 161) Kyra is confronted by José Navidad (p. 164)
	←	2	Cándido helps Al Lopez to build the Mossbachers' fence (pp. 166 ff.)
3			
	↔	4	Kyra (?) presses a few coins into Cándido's hands (p. 201)
5			
	↔	6	Delaney accuses José Navidad of trespassing, but he is distributing Jack's fliers (p. 228)
		7	
8		8	
Part Three			
1			
	→	2	Dame Edith, the cat, joins América as "midwife" (p. 283)
3	→		Delaney attacks José Navidad and is spat at by him (p. 289)
	←	4	Cándido intrudes Arroyo Blanco gardens and steals things (pp. 289 ff.)
5			
	←	6	Cándido kills cat Dame Edith to have some meat for a meal (p. 327)
7	→		Delaney blocks Cándido's path in order to have him arrested (p. 331)
8	↔	8	Cándido, América, Delaney – the final encounters (p. 351 ff.)

The novel is divided into three main parts decreasing in length. These parts have the headings "Arroyo Blanco", "El Tenksgeevee", "Socorro" and show the rough thematic structure of the novel. There is a fairly **symmetrical composition** with 8 chapters for each part and **climactic endings** for each of the three parts. As these climaxes are shaped as real cliffhangers, Boyle succeeds in creating great suspense making the reader read on avidly, or, alternatively, speculate on the open endings (Part One: América's rape; Part Two: Cándido's camp fire gets out of hand; Part Three: América and Cándido are miraculously rescued and Cándido gives Delaney a savior's hand). The three parts as a whole are encircled by a **structural frame interlinking the beginning with the ending**. "It was here, almost at the very spot, that he'd [Cándido] flung himself under the wheels of his car, everything come full circle, and this time Delaney wasn't going to let him off" (p. 332). The initial clash between Delaney as perpetrator and Cándido as victim is mirrored in the ending, when Delaney with gun in hand confronts Cándido and his family. While at the beginning Delaney actually denies human help to his victim, in the very last scene he raises his arm for help which is given to him by Cándido without any hesitation.

The alternating thematic structure of the chapters is underlined by a corresponding alternation in the narrative point of view (see p. 72). The third-person narrator alternately enters the minds of the Americans and the minds of the Mexicans to present their respective stories, views and feelings. In the last chapter the two points of view alternate in fast speed, till both of them, both stories, both lines of action **converge**.
The action of the novel is also structured in a specific **temporal order**. The first part comprises nine days in June giving a detailed account of the two couples' lives spanning from Delaney's accident to Américas rape. The second part speeds up the narrative pace by covering the time from August to Thanksgiving Day (fourth Thursday in November), and the third part again goes into greater detail about the fire, the birth of Socorro, Delaney's man hunt and the final disaster on the day immediately before Christmas. (See the overview in the Appendix: "Alternating Chapters and Temporal Order", pp. 96 ff.)
Although putting the world of the haves and have-nots in stark contrast Boyle avoids the pitfalls of a black and white presentation. The Easterner Delaney emerges mainly as a character distinguishing himself from most of his friends and neighbors as a thoughtful man with a strong feeling of guilt, who at least initially and internally fights against the rising racism in Arroyo Blanco. Likewise the people at the bottom of the social ladder – illegal aliens, Mexicans – do not reveal any solidarity for each other at all; they deeply mistrust and pitilessly victimize each other. There are betrayals, robbery, and sexual attacks. In a harrowing climax at the end of Part One América is

raped by the incarnation of evil, the Mexican José Navidad. He is the novel's vicious wrongdoer tormenting all four protagonists alike. Even the fearless Kyra flinches back from him. "His eyes flashed at her and she saw the hate and the contempt in them, the potential for cruelty, the knowledge and certainty of it" (p. 164).
The structural pattern of the novel which is determined by contrast, juxtaposition, parallelism, interlinking, climactic progession and the all-encompassing frame gives great coherence and poignancy to the story.

The Effect of the Structure

In describing the harrowing strife of the Mexican couple to gain a foothold in American society Boyle creates a story of deep compassion. "Cándido, at first too emblematic, takes on a convincing depth and anger, as – beaten, cheated and derided – he staggers on, indomitably resourceful and improbably honest. América gets work scrubbing statuettes with corrosive cleaner, and is later raped by two syphilitic immigrants. Her sufferings are even more heart-rending than Cándido's, because she – and her baby – are so innocent" (Amanda Craig). In setting this pitiful story in opposition to the self-centeredness, callousness and xenophobia of the privileged people further up the social ladder in Arroyo Blanco Boyle appealingly attacks the deficiencies and injustices of American – and in particular of Californian – society.

2. Plot

The closely-knit structure determines the development of the plot. To critics who find the plot somewhat contrived and predictable, Boyle replies that this is exactly his intention as he wants his novel to be a kind of fable: "I see it as a morality play or a fable and so I've picked extremes. Obviously not everyone is as wealthy as Delaney nor are the illegal immigrants all as desperate as Cándido" (Tom Lappin, "Text Mex", 1995). Clearly the protagonists are meant to be **stereotypes** representing various social attitudes and moral qualities: rich xenophobic Anglo-Americans, poor hard-working, honest but hapless Mexican immigrants, bad and criminal Mexicans, the well-meaning liberal (Todd Sweet), the car dealer being just a car dealer, the helpful American farmer in Oregon, the treacherous rival stealing someone else's wife, Kyra, the one-dimensional, success-oriented realtor, the Eastern liberal Delaney, the indomitable, Job-like Cándido. To a great extent the motives of the characters' behavior evolve from their fixed stereotypes and determine the fairly clear-cut plot. In this context Boyle's ample use of **meaningful names** reinforces his allegorical intentions.

Meaningful names	
Cándido	candid = open, sincere; like Voltaire's Candide he is "the man who bears all the ill luck sent to him" (T.C. Boyle)
América	stands for a borderless America; as a girl with Indian blood she is in some way a native American
Mossbacher	a man living near a brook; *mossback* – a naturalist and conservative who leaves thinking to others
José Navidad	= Joe Christmas , a name strangely unfitting to his character
Todd Sweet	sweet as an ironic comment on a sweetly sounding liberal
Jardine, Cherrystone, Obst, Menaker, Lieberman	European immigrants' names referring to former immigrants who want to have the garden and its fruit denied to new immigrants former European Jewish names
Jack Sr. – Jack Jr	like father – like son
Teófilo Aguadulce	"godloving softwater" – likewise a strangely unfitting name for a man stealing someone else's wife
Al Lopez	a name with both an American and a Mexican element that illustrates his status as an assimilated Mexican-American
Socorro	= "help"; she would have needed it badly; it might be América's outcry
Topanga	Indian word meaning "above"; "the name is an old Shoshonean word and can also be used in reference to the sky or heaven" (Historical Society Topanga)
Arroyo Blanco	white creek

The Sitwells as name givers for Kyra's dogs and cat

Whoever named Kyra's pets, they must have been experts on English literature. Kyra herself? Her first husband?
One may well see in this a satirical jab at postmodernism by the author.

Dame Edith Sitwell (1887–1964): a well-known English poet famous for her tallness and extravagant clothes; she went on a triumphal lecture tour in America in the 1950s
Sir Osbert Sitwell (1892–1969): brother of Dame Edith; poet and writer known for his autobiographical writing
Sir Sacheverell Sitwell (1897–1988): brother of Dame Edith and Sir Osbert; poet and writer known for art and travel books

Delaney's behavior which is initially first determined by a feeling of guilt (for causing an accident, hurting a fellow human being, escaping cheaply, shirking his responsibility, and lying about the cause of his car damage like a hit-and-run guy) and his ideals of liberal humanism gradually degenerate. Events like the car theft, the brushfire spoiling his Thanksgiving festivities, and his humiliating clash with José Navidad bring Delaney's irrational rage and racist tendencies into the open thus propelling the plot to the final showdown. On the whole the ubiquitous José Navidad, his violent transgressions and his potential for evil, play a decisive role in the downturn of the plot by destabilizing all four major characters. Moreover, the two most prominent activists in the "backlash" against the Hispanic aliens, Jack Jardine Sr. and Dominick Flood, contribute to the development of the plot by pulling strings to have the labor exchange closed. In this way they aggravate Cándido's volatile situation depriving him of his only chance to make it in the U.S.A. The ensuing failure of the Canoga Park excursion pushes the Mexican couple another step downwards to doom and despair.

3. Characters

<table>
<tr><th colspan="3">Grouping the Characters</th></tr>
<tr><td colspan="3">Kenny Grisson (car dealer), residents Doris Obst, Bill Vogel, Charlie Tillerman, Kyra's customers and colleagues: the Kaufmans, Paulymans, Matzoobs, Greuterts, Sally Liebermann, Darlene; the two young blokes who give their turkey away; the fat drunk American lady</td></tr>
<tr><td colspan="3">Jack Jardine Sr., Erna – Jack Cherrystone, Selda – Dominick Flood – Jim Shirley
Jack Jr. – his accomplice – American bully ("Elvis hair") – American dog-owner;
Todd Sweet – Oregon farmer</td></tr>
<tr><td colspan="3">Kyra Kit, Orbalina Jordan
Delaney</td></tr>
<tr><td>Asian shop assistants
Indian waiter
Chinese store owner
Italian store owner</td><td>▼
→ TOPANGA ←
▲</td><td>Al Lopez, Señor Willis
Candelario Pérez
Herrera (chicana),
Mexican-U.S. policeman</td></tr>
<tr><td colspan="3">Cándido
América Socorro</td></tr>
<tr><td colspan="3">José Navidad – his companion – Mexican in Canoga – border coyote;
Hispanic workers at the recycling center and Hispanic road workers</td></tr>
<tr><td colspan="3">Resurrección – Teófilo Aguadulce – Cándido's parents, aunt – América's parents
Hilario (Cándido's friend) – Arturio (Hilario's cousin) – two young Mexicans killed
(characters presented in flashbacks)</td></tr>
</table>

3.1 Delaney Mossbacher

Delaney Mossbacher, aged 41, lives the comfortable and well-ordered life of a freelance nature writer. He is five-foot-nine tall (about 1,75 m), weighs a hundred and sixty-five pounds (about 75 kg), he has pale red hair and wears "little lawyer glasses" (p. 17). He is compact, "heavy in the shoulders with a natural hunch that made him look as if he were perpetually in danger of pitching forward on his face" (p. 6). But in case of danger he can display great alertness, the more so as he is in good shape because of his daily hikes.

Note: some reviewers wrongly maintain that Delaney is 39 years old referring to page 114: "Delaney was thirty nine." However, Delaney here remembers his encounter with a young woman he met in a birding class and who tells him about her terrifying experience of being raped in Tujunga Canyon. This meeting took place "just after he'd got to California, before he met Kyra" (p. 114). From another passage we know that he went to California two years before the time of the main action of the novel. Therefore we we can conclude that in July of that year Delaney is 41 years old.

Two years before, he moved from New York to California where he met and married Kyra Menaker, a very successful and efficient realtor. Delaney has been married before, but there is no child as his first wife had an abortion (p. 290). After the divorce from his first wife he was "on his own for eight years" (p. 225). Now with his second wife Kyra, her six-year-old son Jordan, and her beloved pets, Osbert, Sacheverell and Dame Edith, they live in a spacious house on a site of about 6,000 square meters (p. 30) in the private community of the Arroyo Blanco Estates, a comparatively new development high up at the end of Topanga Canyon. As a nature lover Delaney is grateful to have this privileged location of his house. It sits at the end of Piñon Drive, in a cul-de-sac that "marked the last frontier of urban development" (p. 63 f.). From the heights of Arroyo Blanco to the north and east Delaney can see "the San Fernando Valley, a single endless plane of parallel boulevards, houses, mini-malls and streetlights and to the south lay the rest of Los Angeles, ad infinitum" (p. 63). From his garden he can walk straight into the chaparall and the canyons of the Santa Monica Mountains.
Once a month he contributes a column to the nature magazine *Wide Open Spaces*. He has called it "Pilgrim at Topanga Canyon", thus relating himself to the well-known American writer and transcendentalist Annie Dillard who spent four seasons camping out near Tinker Creek, Va. In a health-consuming, obsessive writing process Annie Dilliard put her observations on nature and wildlife in a book she called *Pilgrim at Tinker Creek* (1974) winning the Pulitzer Prize for general non-fiction (1975). Apart from being presumptious in comparing himself to this great writer, Delaney as an agnostic (p. 34) lacks all the religious motivation of Annie Dillard. She tried to find God in nature and thus could rightly call herself a "pilgrim". Delaney "couldn't pretend to her mystical connection to things, or her verbal virtuosity either," but "he did feel that he stood apart from his fellow men and women, that he saw more deeply and felt more passionately – particulary about nature. And every day, from nine to one, he had the opportunity to prove it" (p. 32). The idea of being a pilgrim is so much part of his identity that he even has personalized license plates reading PILGRIM for his fine Acura car. However, his secular pilgrimages to the small wonders of nature gradually lose their attraction, as Delaney enters upon his furious man hunt. Nevertheless he still likes to regard himself as a pilgrim even in this unholy pursuit:

> "All that mattered was this, was finding him, rooting him out of his burrow [...]. Delaney had been here before, been here a hundred times stalking a hundred different creatures – he was a pilgrim, after all." (p. 347)

And "by that time the attentive reader will have recognized that the novel's real pilgrim is not the affluent Delaney who worships 'at the shrine' (p. 76) of nature, but his struggling Mexican antagonist, who wanders through a hostile world in search of a better life and in building makeshift homes for his wife and himself out of the discarded bits and pieces of a throwaway society, becomes a 'pilgrim to build a shrine'" (p. 86; P. Freese, p. 225).

Delaney loves his wife Kyra, is sexually attracted to her, and he shows consideration and compassion. Although he thinks that they have much in common (p. 34), **they differ basically in their general outlooks on life**. Whereas Delaney leads a contemplative life mainly interested in theories like the intrusion and transplantation of species, Kyra has more material and capitalist concerns of how to move real estate objects best. Delaney wears informal dress, Kyra is always dressed up. She regards politeness as essential, whereas Delaney tends to be sarcastic. He is still very much an Easterner in mind, which sometimes irritates Kyra, who is a true representative of the more down-to-earth Western lifestyle. In their sometimes sudden up arguments they become conscious of their differing backgrounds (p. 285).
But their practical arrangements, their **reversing of traditional roles**, suit both. Delaney seems to get along with the housework of cooking, shopping, and supervising Jordan quite well. He is not at all affected by any derisive view of role reversal (p. 35); on the contrary he feels fortunate to be able to enjoy the freedom being granted to him by this constellation. Although she is only mentioned a few times, Delaney's and Kyra's more menial housework is done by their Mexican maid Orbalina. Delaney's relationship to his stepson Jordan is both relaxed and detached. He often ironizes Jordan's habits of TV and play station addiction.
As his parents left him enough money, Delaney is not forced to earn his livelihood and can thus lead the relaxing life of a freelance writer. As soon as Delaney has done his household chores in the early morning, he sits down at his computer and starts to write.

> "This was the moment he lived for, the moment his day really began. [...] he allotted the next four hours to his writing – four hours during which he could let go of the world around him, his fingers grazing lightly over the keyboard, the green glow of the monitor bathing him in its hypnotic light" (p. 32).

In the afternoons he goes out for his hikes in the hills and valleys of the Topanga Canyon area. He is then dressed in shorts, T-shirt and hiking boots, and, careful and efficient as he is, he carries a daypack containing sandwiches, a *bota* bag of water, snakebite kit, sunblock, maps, compass, windbreaker and binoculars (p. 110). In his two years out in the West he has got to know well the area and its native wildlife and flora. Nevertheless, there is still much left to explore.
In social and ethical matters Delaney is described as a "liberal humanist" (p. 3). He is a member of the Democratic Party, he is concerned about the precarious state of environment, and he sees to it that his household waste is recycled. As a student he took part in an anti-nuclear power plant demon-

stration (with his first wife Louise; p. 290). From the beginning we get the picture of a thoughtful, "politically correct" and progessive liberal. When Delaney and his first wife took the agonizing decision to have an abortion, he saw the pro-life protesters on the steps of the abortion clinic as a mob of "hard-line crazies" (p. 290). (See Appendix 2: "Political Correctness – Liberalism – Humanism".)
In spite of being a naturalist and an environmentalist Delaney loves his car, a white Acura Vigor (a Honda car) which he takes great care of. His concern even seems to sometimes surpass his regard for his fellow human beings. After the accident on the canyon road in which he fears he has injured a man, perhaps even fatally, his first thoughts turn to the damage to his beloved car and to his insurance payments. It must be admitted that he reproaches himself for not putting man first: "To his shame, Delaney`s first thought was for the car (was it marred, scratched, dented?), and then for his insurance rates (what was this going to do to his good-driver discount?), and finally, belatedly, for the victim" (p. 4).
The subsequent theft of his car leaves him deeply shaken; there is a constant feeling of loss and insecurity: "He felt violated, taken, ripped off [...]. His stomach clamped down on nothing and the sense of futility and powerlessness he'd felt when he came up the road and saw that empty space on the shoulder flooded over him again" (p. 146) The new car, exactly the same model and color, cannot however completely replace his old companion. The new car must do without the personalized license plates indicating Delaney's deeply felt personal loss. Part of his identity seems to have vanished together with his car.
His first outing with the new car leads him to the Northwestern hills above the ocean. He parks his car along the road and starts hiking down a trail. But the thought of the vulnerability of his car and his craving to protect it condemn him to immobility. He sits down in the brush keeping watch over his car on the road. "He was being paranoiac, that was all – you couldn't hold on to everything, could you?"(p. 155).

Delaney's grandfather immigrated from Bremen giving him the German-sounding family name of Mossbach (probably originating from "Moosbacher" – meaning something like the family living near a mossy stream or brook). On his mother's side there is an Irish grandmother from whom he inherited his red hair ("a pale wispy carrot-top", p. 46). Still aware of his immigrant background Delaney holds to the view of America as a nation of immigrants which is open to everybody (p. 101). In this way he differs from his neigbors who prefer to shut the gates once they have made it in America and have realized their dream.
Similarly, Delaney is first **strongly opposed to the ideas of walls and gates in order to fortify their community**. He thinks that this is an absurd medie-

val thing, contradicting the very idea of America. However, he shrinks back from speaking against the fortifications in public (p. 41). To his mind the gate is a *fait accompli* and moreover, he does not want to be associated with the somewhat strange activists who organize campaigns against the plans. When his wife Kyra becomes a committed campaigner for the wall, Delaney refrains from voicing his resistance publicly in order to save the family's peace and harmony. At the same time his liberal convictions falter under the impression of crime coming up to their secluded place whose very existence was due to the fact that they all wanted to get away from it.

The theft of his car, the girl attacked by "Mexican" or "Armenian" juveniles in Tujunga Canyon (p. 115), Jim Shirley's accounts of burglaries and of the attack on a woman (Sunny DiMandia) in Arroyo Blanco (p. 189), and the incessant crime stories in the inner city sections of newspapers make Delaney reconsider his former convictions. In a kind of sudden revelation "he had a vision then of all the starving hordes lined up at the border, of the criminals and gangbangers in their ghettos, of the whole world a ghetto and no end to it, and he felt the pendulum swing back at him" (p. 227). The naturalist Delaney is especially enraged by the illegal aliens' trash in the canyon. Their camping out, their spoiling and endangering the forests are crimes he personally wants to fight against. It is mainly his fear that hordes of illegal aliens are about to destroy the purity and security of the Santa Monica Mountains which shatter his views and make him step onto the path of a **racist**.

Delaney's turn from muted liberalism to racist hate becomes most obvious in the events of Thanksgiving Day, the day of the fire and the evacuation. Watching the burning fires from the top of the canyon Delaney suddenly sees José Navidad and his Indian companion coming up from the canyon road in a provocative self-assured way. Delaney "felt as much pure hatred as he'd ever felt in his life. What the hell did they think they were doing here anyway, starting fires in a tinderbox? Didn't they know what was at stake here, didn't they know they weren't in Mexico anymore?"(p. 286 f.). The two men are arrested on evidence given by Delaney accusing them of arson although he cannot be sure of this. While they are handcuffed, Delaney feels "a thrill of triumph and hate" (p. 288). When the two alleged arsonists are led away, Delaney and José Navidad for some moments stare at each other in mutual hatred. Just as José is forced to move on by a policeman, he spits into Delaney's face. "The next thing he knew he was on the guy flailing with his fists [...]. "Fuck you!" Delaney roared, and Jack Cherrystone had to hold him back" (p. 289). This is what has become of the peaceful Delaney who has never had a fight since his childhood.

The fact that José and his companion are not guilty of setting the brush on fire and therefore are rightly released demonstrates that Delaney no longer feels obliged to stick to the truth. Under the impression of the heightening events **he jumps to conclusions on the basis of racial prejudice and per-**

sonal feelings of revenge: the already sinking raft of his liberal humanism has gone under. With great zeal and frantic obsession he now tries to prove the Mexican guilty of the graffiti on the new wall. To his great surprise the face on the surveillance photo does not belong to José but to Cándido. In even greater furor Delaney continues his private persecution, concentrating now on Cándido, "his" Mexican. In the end the once considerate liberal humanist and thoughtful naturalist becomes a man hunter who with gun in hand stalks his presumed enemy. But when he is about to get hold of him, he is swept away by the mudslide.

However, throughout the novel Delaney struggles to retain his humanist ideals and liberal attitudes. He cannot be called a downright hypocrite who holds idealistic views but does not live according to them. Whenever he is about to reject one of his beliefs, he experiences an inner conflict feeling anger and shame at the same time and being full of self-reproach: why hasn't he helped the victim of his car accident in true humanitarian spirit? Why does he lie to the car dealer telling him he hit a dog? When he notices his political incorrectness in identifying people by their ethnicity, he is ashamed of himself. His contradictory attitudes and feelings get him into inner struggles. To Kyra's announcement that the 7-Eleven labor exchange has been cleaned up, "Delaney didn't know what to say. He was wrestling with his feelings, trying to reconcile the theoretical with the actual. Those people had every right to gather on that streetcorner – it was their inalienable right, guaranteed by the Constitution" (p. 185). Overhearing the dirty racial jokes of Jack Jr. and his friends about Mexican girls (p. 224) Delaney becomes aware of the effects of walling in a community: this will breed a climate of racism. The wall "might keep *them* out, but look what it keeps in. It was poisonous. The whole place was poisonous, the whole state. He wished he'd stayed in New York" (p. 224f.). He is caught in a catch-22 situation. He does not want to follow his wife, friends and neighbors on their road to racism, but as a recent transplant from the East he is too weak out here to put up an effective resistance. In the end he even outdoes the Westerners with his racist furor.

Grievances, fears and social constraints accumulate in a way that his liberal ideals, his social and ethical convictions, his stings of conscience are gradually suppressed. Delaney changes gradually into an aggressive racist and a "mossback", i.e. a staunch conservative who follows others in their beliefs. (For an overview of Delaney's path from a liberal humanist to a law-and-order racist see p. 111f.) In the same hypocritical and contradictory manner like Jim Shirley, the pro-wall activist who hires the Mexican América to do health-damaging jobs, like Jack Jardine who employs the Mexican José Navidad to distribute the pro-wall fliers in Arroyo Blanco, like Kyra who has Al Lopez and his Mexicans erect the fence, like the Home Owners' Association who have the gate built with the help of Mexican workers, Delaney employs a Mexican maid, Orbalina, "whose English was limited to a response to the six or seven

most common scullery commands" (p. 271). He has adjusted to the **Californian schizophrenia**. Like the Proposition 187 majority he resents the many Mexicans and Hispanics in their midst, but like California as a whole he at the same time relies on Mexicans as cheap labor for menial jobs.
To reconcile this shameful contradiction of having a Mexican maid in their xenophobic house, Delaney and Kyra do not really take note of her as a human being. When the evacuation from the fire is to be considered, Orbalina's thoughts understandably turn to the question of how she will get home to her apartment in the neighboring town Pacoima. No one cares. She is just one of the **invisible workforce** the gringos make use of as 'human capital', but do not recognize beyond this. Only after his traumatic experience of injuring a Mexican with his car does Delaney become aware of the ubiquitous Hispanic workforce with a shock of sudden recognition (p. 11). This is in tune with Jim Shirley, who does not recognize América as a fellow human being. He does not talk to her but gives his orders in gestures and sign language. Furthermore, he uses her as an object for his sexual urges. And Cándido keeps his head down as he walks along the side of the road, "not wanting to risk making eye contact with any of the *gringos* or *gringas* on their way to work in their unblemished Japanese cars. To them he was invisible" (p. 197). "Like Ellison's *Invisible Man* he knows that in the US he is just a disposable non-entity" (P. Freese, p. 230).

3.2 Kyra Menaker-Mossbacher

Kyra, Delaney's emancipated wife, works as a successful realtor for the estate agent Mike Bender in Woodland Hills. She knows the ropes of the trade, she efficiently organizes her day, she is reliable and makes great efforts to establish a special relationship to her customers. "It's the personal touch that counts – and moves property" (p. 36). Her top priority in life is moving estates and everything else is seen functional to it. She works up to 12 hours a day, and even on her way home she checks some of the listed mansions and closes them up for the night. She pays attention to the smallest details of her listings and is obsessed by maintaining a pleasant smell in the unoccupied houses. In this way she means to stress the emotional and sensual factors by which the potential buyers are attracted to a place.
Like Delaney she is very health-conscious. She daily takes twelve vitamins and minerals and keeps in shape by jogging and swimming. She is in her mid-thirties, she has pale blond hair and "see-through eyes" (p. 201). She is always much in command of the situations she has to cope with, and she tackles all tasks with great determination. Together with her fine midnight-blue Lexus car she represents the successful American lady. The Mexicans including Cándido who see her in the streets with her tight skirt, high heels and sunglasses have a less favorable impression of her (p. 201). They cannot help staring at her.

Kyra complains that she does not spend enough time with her son Jordan. His well-being is of great importance to her. When Delaney phones her about his accident, she senses doom before Delaney can say anything. "What's wrong? Is it Jordan? Something's happened to Jordan?"(p. 14). In her marriage with Delaney she often has her way being the dominant partner in the relationship. She has kept her maiden name "Menaker" adding it to "Mossbacher" (we learn near to nothing about her life "before Delaney"). She seeks relief from sorrows and trouble in having sex with Delaney, who does not mind this kind of self-therapy (p. 65).
As an estate agent Kyra watches with great concern the slow infiltration of immigration ills into the once quiet and rural areas. And in one case it is she who takes the initiative to have a labor exchange "cleaned up". Her justification for this takes up the **xenophobic and nativist agenda**: "I agree that everybody's got a right to work and have a decent standard of living, but there's just so many of them, they've overwhelmed us, the schools, welfare, the prisons and now the streets" (p. 185). The solid facts she judges from are less dramatic. She has noticed that at the 7-Eleven parking lot on Ventura Boulevard the number of waiting day laborers has risen from ten to fifty or more. She examines the area around with anger and disgust and is shocked to see that the apartment houses there have degenerated.

> "She didn't see things the way Delaney did – he was from the East Coast, he didn't understand, he hadn't lived with it all his life. Somebody had to do something about these people – they were ubiquitous, prolific as rabbits, and they were death for business" (p. 158).

Ironically enough, mass immigration with its great influx of people to the central areas of L.A. in the past brought **unparalleled estate business** to the outskirts of Los Angeles County, as the well-to-do city dwellers tried to escape from the dirt, noise and disorder of inner city districts and took refuge in areas Kyra specialized in: Calabasas, Topanga, Woodland Hills, Arroyo Blanco. Therefore Kyra first welcomed this development, but now she fears that, if this further outspread is not contained, the immigrant wave will sweep over these once privileged areas and destroy real estate business.
Kyra is much **attached to her pets**, which she has had for quite some time; they are the only ties to her life "before Delaney". She suffers strong shocks when both dogs become prey to coyotes. Keeping out coyotes becomes a major concern to her. First a new and higher fence is erected, and then, after the loss of her second dog, she campaigns for the wall despite Delaney's protest.
Kyra has fallen in love with one of the mansions she is trying to sell and has to look after, namely the Da Roses' home. It is her dream to own such a house once when she will have made enough money to open her own estate agency. After some time the house becomes a refuge for her where she can forget her stressful life and be just herself. To her own surprise she recognizes that

she really does not want to sell this house to anybody. One evening she encounters José Navidad and his companion on the site. Her **determination and assertiveness** in confronting them – and not running away from them – might have spared her América's fate. But this incident, in which she has become terrified as never before, has its lasting effects. Somebody has intruded into her sanctuary and even defaced it by writing PINCHE PUTA ("damned whore") on the wall. Kyra's generally xenophobic reservations about the influx of Mexicans are intensified by her growing anxiety. When it is precisely this house of all her listings that is destroyed by the fire, her nativist sentiments find their strongest expression. Like Delaney Kyra becomes one of the **most outspoken racists**:

> "It was the Mexicans who'd done this. Illegals. Goons with their hats turned backwards on their heads. Sneaking across the border, ruining the schools, gutting property values and freeloading on welfare, and as if that wasn't enough, now they were burning everybody else out too. They were like the barbarians outside the gates of Rome, only they were already inside, polluting the creek and crapping in the woods, threatening people and spraying graffiti all over everything" (p. 311).

At the end of the novel Kyra does not play any role. She seems to have become disillusioned about her job, but on a day shortly before Christmas when she wants to pick Jordan from the home of one of his friends in Agoura, she comes across a dream of a mansion in an area of rural freedom. "Was it still in L.A. County, she wondered, or had she crossed the line?" (p. 337). Kyra obviously has crossed the line in several respects. She realizes that this place could be the starting point for the development of a private community of high-end houses on her own account: "[...] that's where the money was, in developing – not selling – developing" (p. 339). It seems that – beyond the line – Kyra is soon going to be her own boss.

Despite her smaller professional crises and her surprising last move Kyra can be seen as a flat character. Although the reader gets to know her from her own internal perspective, much of her life and character stays in the dark – unless the reader's imagination illuminates it.

3.3 Cándido Rincón

Cándido was born in Tepotzlán in the area of Morelos in the South of Mexico. His father, keeper of a small leather shop, turns his love away from his firstborn son when after the death of Cándido's mother he takes a second wife with whom he has nine children (p. 322). He is only 19 years old when he goes to the U.S. for the first time, working in potato fields in Idaho and in citrus orchards in Arizona. He makes good money there, most of which he sends home. After arriving home at the end of the season he marries Resurrección at the age of twenty. There is a cute little four-year-old flower girl at the wedding, Resurrección's sister América. For seven consecutive years Cándido goes north during the seasons returning home to his wife in the winters. Perhaps because of these long absences, but also because their marriage has not produced a child, Resurrección leaves their house during one of Cándido's absences to live with Teófilo Aguadulce. When Cándido unknowingly returns from the U.S., he has to learn from América that his wife is living with another man in Cuernavaca and is six months pregnant. In a showdown bout with his rival Cándido suffers a humiliating defeat in the presence of all the village people.

This event throws him off the track for five years. To survive he begs from tourists, dances for people in the streets, and presents himself as a street-corner firebreather. He spends all his money on drink and leads a health-depleting life. He finally returns to Teopoztlán to live at his aunt's making some money by producing charcoal. Here he meets América again, falls in love with the lively sixteen-year-old girl, and a year later without getting married they are on their way to *El Norte* together. Their first border crossing fails, when, because of a treacherous "coyote", they are attacked by a gang and then rounded up by the border patrol. They are taken back to Tijuana, where they lead the humiliating life of garbage pickers (p. 18). From there they finally make their way across the border and Cándido leads América to their refuge in Topanga Canyon which he knows from one of his previous stays. "Down here they were safe from all the filth and sickness of the streets, from *la chota* – the police – and the Immigration" (p. 26f.). When Cándido is run over by Delaney – the starting point of the novel's action – they have been living in the canyon for three weeks in which Cándido was hired by two local contractors and earned a few dollars.

Cándido is portrayed as a **Job-like figure** (pp. 121, 353). After his failed marriage with Resurrección almost everything he sets about goes wrong miserably. And also after he has started his new life with América, things turn out wrong in spite of his goodwill, his good character and hard efforts. From the onset of their journey to the U.S. he and América become the victims of various "plagues" making them suffer beyond measure:

- Betrayal of coyote: immediately after crossing the border they are attacked by bandits who take all their money and try to rape América; they are rounded up by the border patrol and América has to stand in line naked.
- Their refuge is destroyed by "right-wing" adolescents.
- América is raped by a countryman. In Cándido's eyes this is his greatest failure for not having been able to protect his young wife.
- Cándido is persecuted by American "devils": Delaney, Jack Jr., "Elvis"-like man.

- Cándido is beaten and robbed by Mexican countrymen in Canoga Park.
- In a brief moment of well-being he forgets his usual circumspection and sets the whole area on fire.
- Cándido's and América's daughter is born blind.
- They are swept away by a flood.

> "[...] he managed finally to curse the engine of all this misery in a burst of profanity that would have condemned him for all time if he hadn't been condemned already. What was it? What was it about him? All he wanted was work, and this was his fate, this was his stinking *pinche* luck, a violated wife and a blind baby and a crazy white man with a gun, and even that wasn't enough to satisfy an insatiable God: no, they all had to drown like rats in the bargain." (p. 353)

Job – the protagonist of the Book of Job in the Bible

Job is a blameless and upright man who fears God and turns away from evil. His life is blessed with wealth and familial happiness. But then he is inflicted with terrible sufferings representing ordeals meted out by Satan to him. He loses all his possessions, all his ten children die at one stroke, **a fire** "is fallen from heaven" and destroys his sheep and servants; he is stricken with a disease which separates him from men. In spite of his laments he does not fall from God and in the end is rewarded for his firmness.

Although Cándido cries out against the **injustice** that the Americans live in abundance whereas he is denied the barest necessities of food, work and shelter, **he does not blame others for his failure**.

> "It was beyond irony, beyond questions of sin and culpability, beyond superstition: he couldn't live in his own country and he couldn't live in this one either. He was a failure, a fool, a hick who put trust in a *coyote* [...], thinking how worthless he was, how unworthy of América, whose life he'd ruined too" (p. 322).

Cándido also falls into despair that the whole area, his refuge, is burned down by a fire he started on account of his personal carelessness. This isn't just bad luck, he feels he has been cursed since the day his mother died. His life is – as even América must recognize – "an ongoing catastrophe" (p. 324).
One can only admire **Cándido's resilience and his willpower** to overcome injuries, betrayals, persecution, hunger, grievances and the inferno of the fire. He suffers degradation and humiliation, he does not hesitate to climb into a leftover container of a restaurant to dig out something to eat. When the fire breaks out, he must collect all his strength to force América to climb to safety. He finds a safe hut and successfully helps her deliver the baby. Soon after that he shrewdly makes use of the absence of the residents to collect

pallets and other material from their grounds to build a new shelter beyond the burned-down one in the brush. Just **like a coyote** he slips out of the gardens before the residents return. He keeps a clear head in critical situations, is unendingly resourceful and indomitable. He toils tirelessly with almost superhuman persistence to assure survival.

Cándido's behavior is determined by the **traditional male role model** of Mexican society. Adhering to hierarchical standards he feels entitled to be the dominant partner in the husband-wife relationship. His male pride is vehemently violated when América successfully insists on trying to get work at the labor exchange. He is ashamed of living on the money his young wife has earned instead of being her provider and protector. In addition, he is greatly concerned about letting her go to places where she is alone with other men. In spite of his deep love towards her he cannot suppress his male aggressiveness and slaps her violently in the course of a heated argument. And when he learns of América's pregnancy he never doubts that his first child will be a son (pp. 24, 181). Cándido is not deeply religious, but in times of distress he seeks consolation in his faith. He prays to "Virgen Sagrada" (p. 55), and his great exhaustion reminds him once of the penitents at Chalma who move ahead on their bare knees for a mile and a half of their **pilgrimage** (p. 17).

As Cándido has been apprehended three times by *La Migra*, the INS police, **he fears nothing more than being caught again and sent back**. This fear makes him and América bear intolerable sufferings. Although twice badly injured he insists on not consulting a doctor. He also prevents América from doing so when there are problems in her pregnancy and when she notices that the baby is blind. In their case the lack of medical care is – under the given circumstances that medical help for illegals exists and he knows about it – self-inflicted because of the towering fear to be detected. To Cándido's mind it is utterly out of the question to return to Mexico however desperate their life is in the U.S.

> "He couldn't go back to Mexico, a country with forty percent unemployment and a million people a year entering the labor force [...]. He couldn't go back to his aunt, couldn't live off her again, butt of the entire village, couldn't face América's parents when he gave her back to them like some precious heirloom he'd borrowed and sullied" (p. 199 f.).

3.4 América

América, the sister of Resurrección, Cándido's first wife, is seventeen years old and like Cándido born in Tepoztlán. She is a beautiful and lively young girl, slim and small, weighing one hundred and five pounds (about 48 kg, p. 28), with shining hair and luminous dark eyes and brown-skinned (p. 59) because of her Indian ancestry (p. 204). She has a well-shaped figure that once

made her attractive to the youths in her village. "[...] she knew she was one of the beauties of Tepoztlán, celebrated for her figure, her shining hair, her deep luminous eyes and her smile that all the boys said was like some rich dessert they could eat with a spoon, bite by bite" (p. 204).
América is the one who as an eleven-year-old girl has to break the news of Resurrección's stealthy departure to Cándido (p. 51). When she is sixteen, Cándido falls in love with her, and on the spot decides to go to the U.S. with her (p. 52) promising her a better life in the "North", "where it was green and lush the year round [...] and everyone, even the poorest, had a house, a car and a TV" (p. 26). Who can resist "the lure of all those things, washing machines, vacuum cleaners, the glitter of the North like a second Eden" (p. 29)? América is caught by her **American dream**, though it is a modest one. It is not "the rags-to-riches" dream, but the hope for a clean white lumber house "and maybe a little yard so you can plant a garden and make place for the chickens" (p. 29).
In contrast to Cándido she can never really come to terms with living in open nature in a makeshift shelter. Her mind is strongly set on an apartment with a clean kitchen, a hot shower and a toilet, "some trees on the street and a market, someplace she could buy a dress, some lipstick, a brush for her hair" (p. 127). While Cándido seems to accommodate himself even with the most primitive conditions, América in heated discussions with Cándido insists on achieving her modest dream. She proves to be persistent and strong-willed, not shying away from a conflict with Cándido. She has her way in going to the labor exchange to find work against Cándido's strong patriarchal resistance. She derives great self-confidence from this successful move, feeling for the first time independent and grown up. She is elated and extremely proud when after her first job she holds her first earned money in her hands.

> "She glowed with the thought of it. She was earning money, money for food, for Cándido and her baby – she, who'd never earned a *centavo* in her life. She'd worked in her father's house, of course, cooking and cleaning and running errands for her mother, and he gave her an allowance each week, but it was nothing like this, nothing like earning a wage from a stranger – and a *gringo*, no less." (p. 92)

América's obstinacy is again evident when she persuades Cándido against his will to spend at least one night in an apartment in Canoga Park. The long walk there, the search for an apartment, being left alone in the street at night, caring for Cándido's injuries, the same long walk back, Cándido's search for food in a leftover food container – all this on top of the great disappointment of not enjoying an apartment for just one night is understandingly too much for her. She withdraws from him blaming him and his incompetence for their desolate situation.

"Cándido was the best man in the world, loving and kind and he'd never known the meaning of the word 'lazy' in his life, but everything he did turned out wrong. [...] It was time to give it up, time to go back to Tepoztlán and beg her father to take her back" (p. 324)

To her the return to the much dreaded camp in Topanga Canyon is the proof of doom and defeat. From then on she withdraws into herself and falls into depression and apathy.
América is closely attached to the **religious culture** of Mexico. She clings to her prayers in times of distress (p. 127), the religious calendar is present in her mind (e.g. The Day of the Dead, p.131), and she deeply pities that she cannot observe the custom of making a pilgrimage to Chalma to hang her baby's umbilical cord in an ancient tree and to pray to the Virgin to give Socorro a long and happy life (p. 325 f.).
With the successful birth of her baby, who is in every living cell and hair a miracle to her, América feels great happiness, fulfillment and pride at being a mother (p. 323). Socorro is "her creation, beautiful and undeniable" (p. 324). This fills her with great satisfaction especially as her parents always doubted she could achieve anything (p. 323 f.). She has left childhood and youth behind; she is a grown-up mother nursing a baby.

3.5 The Two Couples as Contrastive Characters

Delaney	Cándido
does not have to have a job to earn his living	desperately needs a job or any work to survive
his parents leave him a considerable inheritance	his mother dies when he is 6 years old and his father betrays him of his inheritance when he marries a second time
lives in a spacious house in a prestigious well-developed community	seeks shelter in makeshift huts hidden in a canyon
agnostic	religious
is academically educated, enjoys reading nature books and writing, is contemplative and theoretical	has no books, no radio, is left to dreams; has tried to survive as firebreather, street dancer, charcoal maker
can move catlike and alert; aged 41	feels old at 33; has grey hair
likes hiking in canyons as a pastime	has to go on foot up and down the canyons to get to the labor exchange

Delaney	Cándido
considers cooperating with the INS	lives in permanent fear of being turned out of the U.S.A. by the INS; he has been apprehended three times before
does not mind his wife being the main breadwinner of the family; accepts readily a role reversal	is strongly influenced by traditional role models: he feels it is a failure to have to depend on América's work and money

Kyra	América
twice the age of América (mid-thirties), experienced	17 years old, a "child" (p. 28) longs to have her mother to support her
independent and emancipated woman; self-confident, energetic, fearless	dependent on Cándido, unsure, fearful
handles language professionally in her deals which gives her a feeling of superiority	her deficiency in the English language restricts her strongly and makes her reserved
well-shaped, pale blond hair, "see-through" eyes	a slim, well-shaped figure, "tiny" (p. 28), skinny (p. 125), dark-skinned due to her Indian blood (p. 204), dark shining hair, dark eyes (p. 204)
tight skirt and matching jacket, high-heeled shoes	blue cotton dress, *huaraches*
is lucky to be spared from José Navidad's attack	is raped by José Navidad
agnostic	culturally rooted religiousness

3.6 "Minor" Characters

José Navidad	speaks the border Spanish of the back alleys of Tijuana, pale, with eyes "between yellow and red, like twin bruises in his skull (p. 88); his eyes are "jabbing out at the world like two weapons" (p. 81), a *vago* (p. 88); has rotten teeth covered by ill-fitting and cracked dentures; he wears his baseball cap of the San Diego Padres turned backwards (his distinctive epithet); he is intrusive, menacing, ugly, aggressive and cynical in character; syphillitic; it is highly ironic that it is precisely he who should be kept away from all people who distributes the fliers of the Arroyo Blanco wall supporters in Arroyo Blanco

Jim Shirley	Arroyo Blanco resident; imports Buddha statuettes which he has cleaned by illegals in his home; at the same time he is the most outspoken advocate of the wall, stirring up the residents' fear of crime by exaggerated stories and rumors (p. 189); he is the Cassandra of Arroyo Blanco; " a giant of a fat man" (p. 83), a bearded tall man in his fifties who hires América and molests her (p. 97); arrogant and impolite towards América
Jack Jardine Sr.	lawyer, chairman of the Arroyo Blanco Home Owners' Association, head of the campaign for the gate and the wall; an eloquent activist caught up by a siege mentality and strongly opposed to mass immigration
Jack Jardine Jr.	immature adolescent racist harassing Cándido; exchanging racist and sexist jokes with his companion (p. 224)
Jack Cherrystone	a hypocritical but resounding speaker with a voice trained in the nearby film industry
Dominick Flood	Arroyo Blanco resident, rich criminal banker about sixty years old, sun-tanned, white hair; he uses his contacts to have the Topanga labor exchange closed (p. 192); tied to the house by an electronic device for three years because of some business crime; it is ironical that one of the most outspoken activists trying to fend off crime from Arroyo Blanco is a criminal himself; he often entertains; he gives an extravagant Thanksgiving cocktail party; his wife left him some time ago
Todd Sweet	is always dressed in an athlete's clothes; outspoken opponent of gate and wall basing his opinion on the progressive views of the students of the 1960s; he fails to win Delaney for his cause (p. 226)
Al Lopez	Mexican-American building contractor appreciated by Kyra as reliable; employs illegals to replace absent workers
Candelario Perez	Mexican about forty years old, chosen by the workers and employers to keep order at the labor exchange and mediate between the workers and the prospective employers (p. 56)
Jordan	Kyra's son from her first marriage, 6 years old, addicted to Nintendo and television; has to obey his mother's rigid regime of health food
Kit Menaker	Kyra's mother living in San Francisco, fifty-five years old, blond, divorced, coquettish, enamored of Dom Flood who exploits her infatuation to get rid of his electronic shackle

4. Point of View

One of the main distinctive features of fiction (in contrast to factual texts) is a writer's creative configuration of the narrative point of view. In *The Tortilla Curtain* Boyle employs a third-person narrator who assumes a representative role narrating most of the action **through the minds of the four major characters** in a skillful alternating pattern.

So the first chapter presents Delaney's accident from his perspective by narrating the details the way he experienced them and by closely describing his thoughts, emotions and behavior from an **interior point of view**. In contrast the second chapter takes up the action from Cándido's point of view and from a point immediately after the accident, which in Chapter One is set in the middle so that the second chapter overlaps partly with the first. Through Cándido's mind we get to know how miserable he feels and how he manages to get down to his shelter. With Cándido losing consciousness the story is continued by América from her perspective. She finds him lying at the bottom of the path and realizes at once that she is in the worst trouble of her life. After this the reader again follows Cándido`s thoughts, feelings and recollections until the end of Chapter Two.

This pattern of **selective omniscience** in having the two couples and their stories in alternating chapters but in focusing in irregular alternation on one of the four major characters within a given chapter is kept up throughout the novel (see Appendix 1: "Structure in Overview"). In this way we get to know the individual characters from an inner perspective, we learn about what they feel and think and how they participate in the action. With our attention shifting from one character to another we are at first not sure who to give our sympathy to. With the Americans revealing more and more selfish and anti-social attitudes our sympathy will certainly turn to the struggling underdogs, and we will probably feel compassion for the young and innocent victim América.

It is interesting to note that, if passages that cannot or should not be presented through the eyes of one of the four major characters, Boyle's narrator presents the story in **dialogue**. In this way for instance the three Jacks (Jack Jr., Jack Sr., Jack Cherrystone) are given the stage in little scenes mainly consisting of dialogue and direct speech (e.g. Jack Cherrystone's statements at public meetings). Also the quarrels between conflicting partners fittingly take the form of dialogues, so that the squabbles are represented in an unbiased way expressing directly the contestants' points of view. Especially in these scenes the characters come alive and conflicts between them often reach their climax.

In spite of the dominant direct presentation of the characters the **narrator does not hide completely behind them** (as is the case with a self-effacing narrator). The third-person narrator cannot hold back his many satirical comments about the attitudes of the American couple (see "Language – Style – Satire", p. 77 f.). He often interrupts his basic narrative presentation of events and intrudes into the protagonists' experiences. In the case of the Mexican couple the narrator refrains from satire. Their story of toil, blood and tears is told with great compassion. Here the narrator's comments support and enlarge the protagonists' thoughts, often going far beyond the uneducated characters by providing their language and reasoning with implausible versatility and philosophical thought (P. Freese, p. 243).

5. Setting

5.1 Time and Place

The novel, published in spring 1995, was written in the two preceding years. In 1993 and 1994 the hot issue of illegal immigration dominated the political agenda of California. The Californian **Proposition 187** (see p. 15) is only the visible tip of the iceberg. The bitter political debates, the proposition itself and the affirmative vote of November 1994 are not referred to in *The Tortilla Curtain*. However Jack Jardine Sr. is ominously announcing some political action curbing illegal immigration: "We're under siege here – and there's going to be a backlash. People are fed up with this" (p. 146). He might be referring to something political like Propostion 187. Otherwise we find no direct reference to U.S. or Californian politics.

Judging from some details we can rightly suppose that the fictional **story takes place round about that same period**. Delaney's white Acura Vigor GS, which was first produced in 1992 by Honda, has "barely twenty thousand miles on it", when it is stolen (p. 149). Delaney replaces it with the "current year's model", an upgraded version of the Acura Vigor GS, which costs 500 dollars more (p. 146). Therefore one may take the year 1993 as the time in which the novel is set, although the exact year is not mentioned in the text.

(Note: Arroyo Blanco is a six-year-old development which has to follow the 1973 "covenants, conditions and restrictions" [p. 30], the so-called CCRs.)

The actual time of the narration covers seven months from June to December. With flashbacks and recollections of the thirty-three-year-old Cándido it reaches years back to Cándido's childhood in the 1960s extending to his youth and his first years of marriage. The action proper starts on a day at the end of June with Delaney's accident and the first encounter between him and Cándido. In Part One, which comprises nine days, we closely follow the characters almost on a day-by-day pattern. Only nine days after Delaney's car is damaged in the accident, it is stolen from the shoulder of Topanga Canyon Boulevard. In those nine days the narrration grows rather dense: América for example lives through her sorrows about Cándido's serious injuries, she experiences anguishing days among strange "hungry" men, she feels exultation about having earned her first money and she suffers the violent humiliation of being raped.

Part Two encompasses a longer time from July to mid-November considerably speeding up the pace of the narrative after the second chapter. Cándido is hired and fired, the couple undertakes an unfortunate excursion to Canoga Park, the wall is built, and everybody prepares for Thanksgiving (fourth Thursday in November). On the late afternoon of Thanksgiving Day there is the fire alarm ruining everybody's day.

Part Three follows the events immediately after the outbreak of the fire on Thanksgiving Day in a very detailed manner and covers the three days from Thursday afternoon to Sunday afternoon. In a dense sequence of events and an accelerating plot, we first learn about Socorro's birth on Thanksgiving "night" which despite the fire and its devastating menace makes the parents of the new-born baby happy and – befitting the spirit of the day – thankful. The Arroyo Blanco residents are evacuated, Delaney attacks José Navidad; Delaney and his family stay at a hotel for the night, before they can return to their home the following day (Friday). We follow Cándido's endeavors to build a new shelter (Friday morning) and Kyra's despair when she inspects the waste land at the Da Ros place (Sunday). After these climactic events the narrative jumps ahead to the time before Christmas. In a breathtakingly fast finale on one of the days before Christmas, Cándido is hunted down by Delaney and has to learn that his daughter is blind and that his wife was raped. In the end they are all swept away by a giant mudslide and an apocalyptic flood.

Halloween is not mentioned in the novel in contrast to the Mexican **"Day of the Dead"**. This hints at the fact that, with the exception of the lonely and game-addicted Jordan, Boyle refrains from including children in his novel. And the only youths in the book, Jack Jr. and his companion, busy themselves in racist activities and provocations instead of pursuing harmless Halloween pleasures.

It is astonishing how realistically and precisely Boyle creates the place of the action in Topanga and Los Angeles County. You can follow the protagonists' moves with a map in your hand. You can join Cándido and América walking up Topanga Canyon Boulevard and then down to Canoga Park in San Fernando Valley. You can try to find out how Sherman Way has changed in comparison with América's observations (pp. 207–209). You can do business with Mike Bender's and Kyra's counterparts in Monte Nido, Calabasas, Hidden Hills, Agoura Hills or Woodland Hills and keep "a sharp eye" (p. 157) on potential deals along Ventura Boulevard. If you are fed up with hiking in the Topanga Canyon and the neighboring Topanga State Park, you can accompany Delaney to the ocean hills for a change and drive along Stunt Road and Mullholland Drive (p. 154). Coming up the Topanga Canyon Road from

Topanga Beach and Highway 1 you will certainly make a stop at the Topanga post office where the Old Topanga Road turns off left from Topanga Canyon Boulevard. Along Topanga Canyon Boulevard you can "find a lively business community with eclectic stores" (www.woodlandhillsproperty.com). The boulevard leads up the canyon – leaving the **gated community of Summit Pointe** on its right – and runs down to Woodland Hills where you can spend a night or two at the Holiday Inn (p. 291).
The Topanga Summit Pointe gated community does not correspond in size to the fictional Arroyo Blanco Estates with its tennis courts, golf course and 250 homes, although its location might roughly be the same. The houses in Summit Pointe are not the "Spanish Mission style" of Arroyo Blanco (p. 30), but are varied and often imaginative. When creating the fictional Arroyo Blanco Estates, Boyle might have had in mind the plans for a gigantic Summit Valley development which in fights lasting a decade were defeated by the staunch resistance of Topanga citizens. The organizer of this resistance is honored in a monument.
Topanga residents still do without streetlighting – just as we know it from the novel. In spite of the ever-increasing commuter traffic Topangans have successfully turned down repeated plans to restructure the canyon road to give it four lanes.
Trash in the canyons – "American trash" like cars, refrigerators and the like – is still a big problem, and there are yearly cleanings by volunteer and school initiatives. The return of former species – fish, birds and plants – is publicly celebrated by the nature-oriented community. Delaney as a naturalist and environmentalist is extremely furious at the trash he comes across in Topanga's canyons. He blames the pollution of nature on the illegals who hide and camp out there. When Cándido frantically looks for a place to climb up out of the burning canyon he finds a garbage dump, a slope of refuse towering up to a precipice, from where "generations of heedless *gabachos*" have hurled their junk down into the valley (p. 276). He is certainly not in the mood to realize that by climbing up over the gabachos' junk – cars, toasters, water heaters, bedsprings – they are able to rescue themselves from the fire. The reader is reminded of Cándido's reflections when "he was stalled in the garbage dump in Tijuana [...]. *Life is poor here*, an old man – a garbage picker – had told him. Yes, he'd said, and he was saying it now, the words on his lips somewhere between the two worlds, *but at least you have garbage*" (p. 18).

In 1771, twelve years before the city of Los Angeles was founded, Spanish settlers established the **San Gabriel Mission** in the area which is now Topanga. However, it was not until 1885 that the first residential houses were built here. Deliberately leaving realism behind, Boyle makes ample use of Spanish vocabulary and allusions to the Spanish past in his description of Topanga's gated community. It is called Arroyo Blanco ("white creek"), the

private streets, the Vias, Calles and Avenidas (p. 225) in Arroyo Blanco carry Spanish names: "Piñon Drive", "Arroyo Blanco Drive", "Via Dichosa", "Via Mariposa", "Via Esperanza", "Via Dolorosa". And the prescribed architectural style of the houses is that of the "Spanish Mission style" (see picture on p. 18). It is of course highly ironical and part of Boyle's satire that the private American development, which is specically designed to fend off Hispanics, indulges in the Spanish and Mexican tradition of California.
The **symbolical contrast of the locations of the couples' homes** is expressed by situating Delaney's house and Arroyo Blanco high up in the mountains above Topanga (Topanga meaning "above") and making Cándido seek refuge deep down in the canyon beside a creek. Cándido's and América's hiding place in the canyon turns out to be an almost deadly trap from which they have only a very narrow escape. They frantically leave everything behind (even their only money buried in the ground) and climb up rocks and steep slopes (p. 275). By contrast Delaney and Kyra, whose home is eventually spared from the fire, are evacuated, but have enough time to load their car with their most precious belongings.

5.2 Socio-political Background

Although the novel had and still has reverberations in the political debate, Boyle insists that *The Tortilla Curtain* is **not a political novel** in the strict sense. He is not so much interested in the political aspect of illegal immigration and the pros and cons of Proposition 187 measures, but in **the social climate that has led up to the controversial immigration policies**. It is Boyle's strength to focus on the social conditions of rising xenophobia and to narrow down the view on a locally and socially restricted entity. As in *East is East*, *The Road to Wellville*, and *Drop City* the reader is confronted with the attitudes and social dynamics of an insulated group of people who feel endangered by the intrusion of aliens. The Arroyo Blanco community serves Boyle as his limited social group for "a case study in the genesis of xenophobia" (P. Freese, p. 221).
It is the **socio-psychological aspect of fear** – fear of losing ground to intruders, fear of becoming victims of crime, fear of public disorder, fear of getting third-world situations –, and the **aspects of group pressure, conformity and moral integrity** that Boyle is interested in. In *The Tortilla Curtain* he certainly wants us to note the wider **socio-demographic context** in which the action of the novel is set. There are of course the record numbers of immigrants who leave a strong impact on economic, social and cultural life in North America. And there is the "native-born" population who in part feel encroached upon and – in Jack's words – "under siege" (p. 146). The demographic change determines the social climate of apprehension, insecurity and fear. It is characterized by "the charged relationship between a shrinking

white majority that feels increasingly beleaguered and a number of steadily growing ethnic minorities that are clamoring for recognition" (P. Freese, p. 221). One of Boyle's intentions with the novel lies in his warning that such a climate is the breeding ground of racism.

6. Language – Style – Satire

Critics agree that with *The Tortilla Curtain* Boyle has departed from his usually exuberant, witty and highly amusing style. This novel is not fanciful or funny but fitting in with the seriousness and social urgency of its subject matter. Boyle makes use of "a stripped-down, dead-sober tone" (David Eggers, *San Francisco Chronicle*, September 10, 1995).
The story is too deadly serious to give room for good-natured humor and witty irony. The most striking stylistic element of the novel is bitter **satire**. With all his verbal power Boyle satirizes the American characters, major and minor ones without distinction. The continuous sarcasm and ridicule exposes the Americans' selfishness and hypocrisy and makes them appear unlikeable and unsympathetic to the reader.
Even on the first page we are confronted with **sarcasm** when the male American protagonist is introduced "as a liberal humanist with an unblemished driving record and a freshly waxed Japanese car with personalized plates" (p. 3). A deeply critical attitude towards the American characters emerges throughout the whole novel. Delaney "was in a rage, and he tried to calm himself. It seemed he was always in a rage lately – he, Delaney Mossbacher, the Pilgrim of Topanga Creek – he who led the least stressful existence of anybody on earth besides maybe a handful of Tibetan lamas" (p. 154). Kyra is equally exposed to sarcasm: "real estate was her life" (p. 35); "for Kyra, sex was therapeutic" (p. 65). In real estate business Kyra thinks that it is "goodwill, that's what counted. [...] And when the time came to list their property, they [people in her area] would go to Kyra Menaker-Mossbacher, the empress of goodwill" (p. 156). While some critics see here an effective means of criticism directed at the self-centred Americans, others are taken aback by the obvious and deep **contempt for American characters**. "Contempt is a dangerous emotion, luring us into believing that we understand more than we do. Contempt causes us to jeer rather than speak, to poke rather than touch. Despite his celebrated gifts, T. Coraghessan Boyle may be the most contemptuous of our well-known novelists" (Scott Spencer, *New York Times*, September 3, 1995, Late Edition).
Nevertheless, also in *The Tortilla Curtain* Boyle is brilliant in his **language**. Its main features are an extremely rich vocabulary especially in the fields of food, animals and plants, an outstandingly varied choice of words, a lucid and propelling syntax, and a powerful imagery that exudes inventiveness

and originality. "Mr. Boyle is first-rate in capturing the terror of looking for work in an alien society" (Scott Spencer), as in the passage describing Cándido's experience at the labor exchange, the post office parking lot:

> "And then the contractors began to arrive, the white men, with their big *bleached faces* and soulless eyes, *enthroned* in their trucks. They *wanted* two men or three, they *wanted* four or five, *no* questions asked, *no* wage stipulated, *no* conditions or terms of employment. A man could be *pouring* concrete one day, *spraying* pesticide the next – or *swabbing* out urinals, *spreading* manure, *painting*, *weeding*, *hauling*, *laying* brick or *setting* tile. *You* didn't ask questions. *You* got in the back of the truck and *you* went where they took you." (p. 129; italics by K.E. Sch.)

One may have scruples to analyze the style of this impressive passage for fear of destroying its impact, but the following elements should be noted: similes, instances of repetition, parallelism, gradation, ellipses and enumeration. Critics ironize Boyle's stylistically loaded prose: He "is the **m**aestro of **m**etaphors, the **s**ultan of **s**imiles, and, oh yes, an **a**ficionado of **a**lliteration" (Barbara Nachman, "Hometown Rebel", *The Journal News*, November 12, 1998). Here is another example of Boyle's narrative style in the description of Delaney at the very beginning:

> "Immediately, before he could even *catch* his breath, he was *brushed* back by the tailwind of a *string* of cars *racing* bumper-to-bumper up the canyon *like some snaking malignant train*. He clung to the side of his car as the sun *caught his head in a hammerlock* and the un-air-conditioned heat rose from the pavement *like a fist in the face*, like a knockout punch. Two more cars *shot* by. He was dizzy. Sweating. He couldn't seem to control his hands. 'I've had an accident,' he said to himself, repeating it over and over like a mantra, 'I've had an accident.'"(p. 4; italics by K.E. Sch.)

The imagery (metaphors and similes) as well as the varied sentence patterns help the reader feel the devastating effect of the accident. Delaney is attacked by the traffic, the heat, the sun and by a dreadful situation he has never been in. We will not be surprised to learn that such an extraordinary and unsettling incident will have lasting effects on the further course of his life.

7. Topics – Motifs – Symbolism

7.1 Nativism in Arroyo Blanco

At the outset of the novel the liberal Delaney would harshly repudiate any kind of nativism or xenophobia. Judging from his proclaimed ideological views he would stand for an open multiracial society represented by the U.S.A. as the traditional nation of immigrants and its famous Statue of Liberty welcoming immigrants without any reservations. (For Delaney's "liberal creed" see p. 111.)
With his high-minded views however, Delaney is alone among his neighbors and friends and even gradually isolated from his wife. So it is only a matter of time and circumstances before his liberal attitudes crumble. As a newly-arrived writer from the East he is not firm enough to uphold his convictions against the collective xenophobia of his wife, his neighbors and even his car dealer out there in the West.
When we blend their views together, we arrive at an almost complete catalogue of the political **nativist** agenda (see Appendix 3: "Nativism in the U.S.A."):

- Hordes of immigrants continuously pour in from Mexico and Central America, display a birthrate of "prolific rabbits" and overwhelm native-born Americans (Kyra; p. 107).
- They overcrowd the public schools, deplete the welfare budgets, fill the prisons and loiter in masses in the streets which are beginning to "look like fucking Guadalajara or something down there" (Jack Cherrystone; p. 192).
- Their culture is inferior, resembling that of barbarians (Kyra; p. 311).
- With the influx of immigrants crime is imported even far out to the once quiet and wealthy communities in the Santa Monica Mountains. There are brazen break-ins and cruel attacks on women (Jim Shirley; pp. 43, 188, 189).
- Car thefts are everyday events and part of organized crime; in this way people in Mexico are provided with American luxury cars. Criminality is "pervasive as death" and this is not only to be blamed on the Mexicans, but also on the "Salvadorians, Iranians, Russians, Vietnamese" (Kenny Grissom; p. 147).
- Society as a whole has deteriorated (Jack Cherrystone, Jack Jardine; pp. 11, 44), and it can only be restored, if immigration is drastically restricted and, above all, if illegal immigration is cracked down on. The technologically far-developed American economy has no jobs for those "farmhands" coming through the Tortilla Curtain without education, skills or resources, the more so as California has "a ten percent unemployment rate – and that's for citizens" (Jack Jardine; p. 101, Jack Cherrystone; p. 192).

- Illegals turn in taxes only a fraction of the sum that is spent on them in schools, welfare and medical care. On top of that they do not spend their money in the U.S.A., but send most of it home thus withholding it from the American economy (Jack Jardine: p. 102).
- It is foolish to assist them in the form of labor exchanges and the like: "the more you give them the more they want, and the more of them there are" (Bill Vogel; p. 192).
- The suburban sprawl overwhelming and destroying once idyllic communities is the result of mass immigration. The once pristine nature has become insecure and degraded by the trash of illegal aliens (Delaney; passim).

A Nativist Cartoon

Political correctness at the Tortilla Curtain

The debates around Proposition 187 aroused blatant nativism in California. In the cartoon opponents of the proposed measures who maintain that basic humanitarian rights need to be granted to everybody are sarcastically ridiculed as people attempting to rob native-born Americans to give the money to Mexicans.

Some nativist arguments (e.g. strain on local budgets and welfare) do refer to undeniable facts, but the whole doom-spelling scenario of nativism is greatly exaggerated and not so much based on actual facts as on people's vague fears. Sociologists maintain that American nativism has less to do with the phenomenon of immigration than with the state and psyche of American society. They hold that nativist sentiment has been highest when the nation's problems were and have been "so intractable that some people seek scapegoats. Typically, these periods feature a political and economic crisis, combined with a loss of faith in American institutions" (James Crawford, "Cycles of Nativism in U.S. History", National Immigration Forum 2001).
The nativism in Arroyo Blanco is mainly based on the fear that the ills of metropolitan Los Angeles may endanger the residents' privileged lifestyle. Under the supposed encroachment and intrusion of the "aliens" they get together and try to fend off that imminent danger. With an assumed intrusion coming fom outside the cohesion within increases, and the home owners attend the community meetings in great numbers. Only now, after two years, does Delaney come into closer contact with some of his neighbors at these meetings (pp. 42, 187).

7.2 Cars and Traffic

The richness in detail concerning cars and traffic is one of the striking features of the novel thus commenting on the great importance cars have in American society. They are treasured possessions, status symbols, "ciphers of wealth" (p. 200) and playthings. Delaney is in love with his white Acura Vigor GS and keeps it in immaculate condition. The comparatively minor damage stemming from his crash with Cándido has to be rectified immediately. His car has to be in a state of cleanliness and perfection, and Delaney is overcome by great unease when he is forced to give up his symbiosis with his car. Handing the key over to a parking lot attendant, who – on top of it – is a Mexican, means depriving him from part of his identity and command over his life. After the theft of his car the fear of being again separated from his volatile possession and of losing it paralyzes him. The car as the American symbol of freedom and mobility seems to enslave Delaney.
However, when at the end the frenzied fever of man hunt gets hold of him, he disregards his usual care for "his new milk-white Acura Vigor GS with the tan leather upholstery and only thirty-eight hundred and sixteen miles on the odometer" (p. 333). He forgets all precaution and carelessly risks an accident which badly damages his brand-new car. While after his first accident his confused thoughts instinctively turned to his car, here Delaney at once turns to his "victim" and "prey": he commands Cándido to stay where he is. He makes a 911 phone call not because of the accident, but in order to have Cándido arrested.

Kyra's dark-blue Lexus matches her overdone elegance and stands for her personal success. Like her uniform-like dress the luxury car is part and parcel of her job: "She was all business, bright and chirpy, dressed in property-moving best, the Lexus a massive property-moving tool" (p. 244). To both Kyra and Delaney their cars are a kind of refuge, a "sanctuary" (p. 73) where they find peace and safety against the hubbub of the outside world (see p. 9: "sealed in and impervious once again"; p. 335: "it gave her a cozy feeling, a feeling of being impervious to the elements, sealed in and secure").
Beside his Range Rover Jack Jardine Sr. has got as a weekend plaything a "classic 1953 MG TD"; Jim Shirley has a "rich new car" (p. 94) with a luxurious interior (p. 83); and there are Land Rovers, Mercedes-Benzes and Jeep Cherokees of other Arroyo Blanco residents documenting their status and wealth. By contrast, the eccentric Señor Willis has an old dilapidated Corvair which hardly manages to get up the canyon road (p. 251), and Cándido and his countrymen buy a rusted-out 1971 Buick Electra to get from Idaho to California (p. 167), which breaks down after the first few miles.

The once idyllic Topanga Canyon Road has to suffer from the onslaught of the cars, especially during rush hours. The urbanization of the San Fernando Valley and of the communities along Ventura Boulevard have brought never-ending commuter traffic up and down the canyon road. Overpopulation and the proverbial American restlessness, the Americans' chase for money and wealth, are seen as the causes of the traffic congestion in the once peaceful rural areas. To Cándido the busy canyon road traffic is a "crazy gringo tail-light-chasing rush – and what was the hurry, the constant hurry? Making a buck, that's what. Building their glass office towers and adding up the figures on their dark little TV screens, getting richer – that's what the hurry was. And that's why the *gabachos* had cars" (p. 91). Besides Cándido, also América and Delaney suffer from the crazy traffic (p. 56, p. 111, p. 119). In contrast Kyra has adapted to these conditions and can flow with the traffic, literally and metaphorically speaking: "Traffic was traffic, and it didn't faze her a bit. She moved with it, sat in it, ran with its unfathomable flow" (p. 73).
Once people have left their cars or are left alone outside, they seem to fight a losing battle. Throughout the novel there is an abundance of similes portraying the car as a weapon, even in Delaney's point of view: "One after another the faces of the drivers came at him, shadowy and indistinct behind the armor of their smoked-glass windshields" (p. 5). The cars in Kenny Grierson's showroom are "hard and unassailable" (p. 13) to him. Cándido stands no chance in this unequal fight: "All that steel, that glass, that chrome, that big hot iron engine – it was like a tank coming at him, and his only armor was a cotton shirt and pants and a pair of worn-out *huaraches*" (p. 17). And Kyra is in great danger of being attacked, when she walks alone over the lawn of the Da Ros place.

7.3 Borders – Boundaries – Territory – Intrusion

Intrusion into alien territorries in spite of borders, boundaries, preventive measures, and fending off intrusion – these are major recurrent and varying motifs in *The Tortilla Curtain*.
Because of the immense economic differentials between Mexico and the U.S.A. no boundary whatsoever – neither the corrugated iron fence at Tijuana (p. 59) nor the Rio Grande and the desert – will deter the desperate people from the poor South from going to the North to pursue their American dream. The Mexican-American border, especially the stretch of the so-called Tortilla Curtain is a place of horror to the Mexicans, but a symbol of weakness and political failure to the American characters of Boyle's novel.
At the Tortilla Curtain Cándido and América have experienced the treachery of "coyotes", rape and robbery by countrymen ("vagos", "animals"; p. 59), the ruthlessness of the border police, the filth in Mexican border towns. The term Tortilla Curtain stands for all this. To many Americans like Jack Jardine Sr., for example, the Tortilla Curtain is mainly a symbol of ineffective control, of putting Border Patrol officers in a no-win situation and of plunging the hinterland into disorder. To them restoring law and order in the L.A. area will only succeed, if "we get control of the borders" (p. 101), and in their eyes it is a question of national sovereignty to regain command over the border and people crossing it. They demand that illegal immigration has to be ended by closing up the gaps in the Tortilla Curtain. "The ones coming in through the Tortilla Curtain down there, those are the ones that are killing us" (p. 101).
Delaney, who is well aware of the Spanish past, does not fail to see the irony that in a way some kind of **reconquista** of the Spanish territory is going on: "we'd stolen California from them in the first place" (p. 102). When discussing the graffiti on the new Arroyo Blanco wall – which has in fact been daubed by Jack Jr. – Kyra claims that you can see these signs all over the valley as some kind of secret code. Whereupon – ironically enough – Jack Sr. ventures into the animal world to find an explanation: "'It's like an animal reflex, isn't it? – marking their territory?' 'Only this is our territory,' Kyra said." And in rather an ambiguous comment Delaney adds: "'I wouldn't be so sure'" (p. 316 f.).
Pushing into new territories, trespassing, trying to prevent people and animals from intruding, chasing people off one's property is mirrored in various facets throughout the novel:

- illegal aliens intruding into "Delaney's" nature and canyons;
- coyotes intruding into housing areas;
- the (Hispanic) "invasion from the South", i.e. mass immigration into Southern California and L.A.;
- "urban life" (p. 153) with all its nastiness is intruding into the communi-

ties of the Santa Monica Mountains ("Why don't you just fuck off, lady", p. 153);
- urban crime violates the peace of nature: hikers with guns, robberies, rape on canyon trails, shooting exercises in the woods."The city was here, now, crouched in the ravine" (p. 114);
- day laborers and loitering immigrants swamping formerly "orderly" residential areas along Ventura Boulevard;
- José Navidad intruding into Kyra's sanctuary: the Da Ros place;
- the coyote stalking pets in Delaney's and Kyra's garden;
- putting up a fence against coyotes and snakes;
- the closure of the labor exchange: ALL PERSONS WARNED AGAINST TRESPASS" (p. 198);
- an ominous looking car prowling through Arroyo Blanco menacing its peace and tranquility;
- retrofitting Arroyo Blanco with gate and wall;
- Delaney feels that Cándido has "invaded" (p. 332) his life like some parasite, and as he is unwilling to be the victim of this invasion he strikes back;
- the intrusion of the "primitive" Mexican lifestyle into the refined lifestyle of privileged Americans: "naked children, pigs, cookfires [...] she could not have that. Not here" (p. 163).

The community's fortifying efforts have annihilated Delaney's much appreciated local and symbolical position on the borderline between civilization and nature. "His house sat at the end of Piñon, in a cul-de-sac that marked the last frontier of urban development" (p. 63 f.). The new wall shuts him off from nature and robs him of part of his identity thus causing alienation: "He was being walled in, buried alive, and there wasn't a thing he could do about it" (p. 244). His wife's present, the stepladder, only finds his sarcasm; it is a symbol of a ridiculous attempt at bridging his separation from nature.
At the end of the novel Kyra leaves her territory and at the same time the scene of the action. When fetching her son Jordan from a schoolmate's home she somehow gets into an area unknown to her. "Was it still in L.A. County, she wondered, or had she crossed the line?"(p. 337). She obviously has crossed it in a concrete and symbolic sense. She has entered new territory. Far out there beyond the Comada Canyon in the Agoura hills she comes across a huge house in wide open spaces which is up for sale by the owner. Being fed up with her small scale selling job she is ready to begin something new in her real estate career. She cannot resist driving up to the huge mansion: "she was thinking about the adjoining properties and who owned them and whether this place could be the anchor for a very select private community of high-end houses, and that's where the money was, in developing – not selling – developing" (p. 339). And with these capitalist thoughts Kyra leaves the scene.

7.4 Coyotes

The coyote is the central leitmotif of the novel appearing in various shades of meaning. The term "coyote" has become the informal but popular word for the **Mexican scout who organizes and guides the border crossings of illegal immigrants** through the Tortilla Curtain for money. Their reputation has been blemished by some who commit acts of violence, robbery and betrayal. If you consider the animal's amazing qualities, the term coyote is aptly chosen to show the ambivalence of these men's activities. Coyotes are generally considered to be sly, cunning, unstoppable, unpredictable in their movements. As we know from the novel, the coyote can stupendously scale walls and fences, it is described by the expert Delaney as "our cleverest and most resourceful large predator, the creature the Indians apotheosized as the Trickster" (p. 211). But pitifully enough it takes man's dearest pets as prey, and it does not shrink back from attacking babies lying unguarded in their cots in the gardens or patios.

The coyote is a generally accepted **symbol of pre-Columbian America** and it appears in manifold forms and roles in North American Indian myths. It is an indigenous animal of North America, and its habitat is as wide-spread as the continent. It was living freely in its territory long before the white settlers came and curtailed its once unrestricted space. In his articles the naturalist Delaney sees the struggle between man and coyote in the light of the broad perspective of natural history in which in Darwinian fashion man and animal alike fight for territories to assure survival. "After all, the coyote roamed these hills" long before man appeared there, and "if we invade his territory, then why indeed should we surprised when he invades ours?" (p. 212). To check the annoying intrusion of the coyote in residential areas Delaney pleads to people not to invite the clever and adaptable coyote with leftover food, pet food and the like in and around their properties. To him it is out of the question to trap, shoot or otherwise decimate the coyote, above all because this is useless. Its extreme adaptability, its flexible adjustment to changing conditions will guarantee its survival. If you try to eradicate the animal, the coyote population "will simply breed up to fill in the gap, the bitches having litters of seven, eight or even more pups […]. The coyotes keep coming […], moving in where living is easy. They are cunning, versatile, hungry and unstoppable" (p. 214 f.).

One cannot but notice the intended **parallels between the coyotes and the illegal Mexicans** in California. Jack's remark about the animal instinct of illegal Mexicans marking their American territory is obvious evidence of this (p. 316). When Kyra spots something moving in the grounds of the Da Ros place, she instinctively thinks of a coyote. Symbolically enough, the coyote turns out to be the ubiquitous **José Navidad** who has much in common with the elusive animal.

In his resourcefulness and ingenuity to find means to survive **Cándido** also resembles the coyote in a positive sense. When building the shelter for América and their baby Cándido several times scales the wall to fetch what he needs. Parallel to the coyote who stalks and takes Osbert and Sacheverell as prey, Cándido lures Kyra's remaining pet Dame Edith and takes advantage of his predatory superiority in the struggle for survival.

The reader will understand much of Delaney's reflections on the coyote as a comment on Mexican immigration. In his elaboration of themes like transplantation, adjustment and survival of species as well as "population conflict" (p. 241) Delaney clearly has not only the described animal in mind. Within the framework of his Darwinist views Delaney is only consistent when he considers Kyra's and Dom Flood's attempts at "cleaning up" the labor exchanges of the Mexican day laborers as futile. "But where were these people supposed to go? Back to Mexico? Delaney doubted it, knowing what he did about migratory animal species and how one population responded to being displaced by another. It made for war, for violence and killing" (p. 193).

The coyotes' and the illegal aliens' intrusion can in Delaney's view only be answered by the adjustment of American society. The Mexicans' and in particular Cándido's readiness to endure suffering, to get on with very little, and also their inventiveness to somehow ensure their survival, their adjustment to a hostile environment, their resourcefulness to find niches in American society are all qualities in which the coyote and the Mexicans excel. The novel even hints at a resemblance in the high fertility rate, which has to be seen however in the context of Kyra's racist prejudices (p. 158).

Both the coyote and the Mexican seem to want something back from the cake they were deprived of by the Americans. The residents gathered at Dom Flood's house probably do not see the dramatic irony of their seemingly funny joking. When they hear the coyotes barking in the hills, giving signals to each other almost as a call to arms, Jack Cherrystone rumbles: "'The natives are getting restless,' [...]. 'You think they want to come and join us?' Bill Vogel said. [...] 'They probably get a little tired of raw rat or whatever they're eating out there – if I was a coyote I'll bet a bit of this cheesecake would really hit the spot'" (p. 191).

Finally there is **América's identification with the coyote** in one of her day dreams. One afternoon, a coyote interrupting her boredom approaches her near their camp. She can only see the ideally camouflaged animal, when she cocks her head "the magic way" (p. 178).

> "It was a coyote. Bristle fur, tanned the precise shade of the dried hill grasses, one paw lifted, ears high. [...] She looked at that coyote so long and so hard that she began to hallucinate, to imagine herself inside those eyes looking out, to know that men were her enemies [...] and she saw the den full of pups and the hills shrunk to nothing under the hot quick quadrupedal gait" (p. 178 f.).

7.5 Fire and Flood

The area's environmental vulnerability to natural disasters stems from climatic factors and geological conditions. Great aridity in summer and fall, the hot Santa Ana winds, and the dry brush favor the outbreak of the much dreaded fires. Delaney is still taken aback by the hot Californian falls:

> "But here, in the bleached hills above Los Angeles, fall was just another aspect of eternal summer, hotter, drier, hurled through the canyons on the breath of winds that leached all the moisture from the chaparral and brought combustible oils to the surface of every branch and twig" (p. 240).

The constant threat of fire in the Santa Monica Mountains have forced the people and public bodies to establish a strict regiment of precautionary measures from simple rules for proper conduct in state parks to wide-ranging emergency measures like the evacuation of whole communities. The fact that a petty act of carelessness can ignite a devastating firestorm destroying valuable properties in vast areas is much present in Delaney's mind. In summer the canyon and its hills are "a tinderbox" (p. 11), and his outrage turns against people who camp there although it is strictly forbidden. The 'Thanksgiving fire' caused by Cándido's carelessness is repeatedly **foreshadowed**. So for example we learn from Delaney that the previous year's firestorm was obviously caused intentionally by a pyromaniacal arsonist (p. 111).
Fire as a **destructive force** to man and nature is contrasted with the **rejuvenating and purifying, enriching effects** it has in nature. "The canyon had already recovered, and he [Delaney] noted with satisfaction […] the abundance of vegetation that would succeed it [the blaze]. Fertilized by ash, the grasses and wildflowers had put out a bumper crop, and the hills stood waist-deep in stiff golden grass, all part of the cycle, as undeniable as the swing of the earth over its axis" (p. 111).
"Cándido's fire" ironically raging on Thanksgiving Day 'destroys' the festivities of the Americans and the very first signs of the returning good mood between Cándido and América. In seemingly unjust manner the fire devastates the Mexican couple's shelter and "eight redwood cabins just to the south of Arroyo Blanco in a little enclave of people living alternative lifestyles – hippies, bikers, palm readers, New Age enthusiasts and the like" (p. 292), but it leaves Arroyo Blanco unscathed. It is spared from the fire, because the Santa Ana winds die down with the approaching night. However, as if to demonstrate its impartiality, the fire devastates Kyra's dream and secrete refuge, the Da Roses' mansion.

Rain and water – usually symbols of fertility – are mainly presented as destructive forces. The sudden incessant rains in early winter cause floods and mudslides on the dried-out mountains, and especially where recent fires

have destroyed forests and trees, the torrents of rain are the cause of uncontrollable erosion and water flow. In the final chapters of the novel the frequent reference to the torrential rains and soaked hillsides (pp. 317, 319, 326) function as **premonitions and foreshadowings** of the impending disaster. "But that was always the way: after the fires, the rains, and the rains brought their own set of complications" (p. 314). The creeks in Topanga Canyon then become wild torrents, and Cándido has presentiments of a menacing tragedy. Hanging around the post office in the hope of being hired for the day he "could hear the creek where it cut into the bank out back of the post office before whipping round to pass under the bridge and plunge into the cut of the gorge. It was a sinister sound [...]. They would have been flooded out if they were still camped below, flushed down the canyon like waste in a toilet" (p. 329).
The huge mudslide and the apocalyptical flood just before Christmas are enormous and must have done immense damage to the canyon. The narrator however sticks to his restricted focus and perspective and limits the action to what happens to Cándido, América, Socorro and Delaney, i.e. to what they experience when they are swept away. Some readers critically reacted to the seemingly improbable and exaggerated role given to nature in the ending. To the detriment of Californians Boyle has been only too realistic in depicting this final natural disaster.

Fire and Flood: Recent Disasters

- In 2003 there was a disastrous fire siege which destroyed more than 3,600 homes in Southern California.
- Torrential rains came down on the Santa Monica Mountains for several days from Jan. 6 to Jan. 11, 2005. A mother lost her 2-year-old girl, who slipped in the flood, got loose from her mother's grasp and disappeared with the torrent.
- A 25-foot boulder came down on Topanga Canyon Road blocking it for days.
- Heavy rains caused various mudslides blocking roads in the Santa Monica Mountains. On Jan. 10, 2005, a huge mudslide sluiced down the mountain above the seaside town of La Conchita. It rumbled down the hill carrying trees, debris and mud all over the town. Many people were swept under the wave of mud and killed.

7.6 Food

Food is a graphic and sensual feature helping create the contrast between the two worlds contrasted throughout the novel. Cándido and América can buy only small amounts of inexpensive food, but they enjoy and savor their tortillas, tomatoes and beans. It strikes Cándido as strange that in spite of the abundance in supermarkets food is robbed of its original smell and condition by wrapping it in and sealing it off. The Americans "sanitized their groceries

[...] and drove life from everything, imprisoning their produce in jars and cans and plastic pouches, wrapping their meat and even fish in cellophane" (p. 122 f.).

The Mossbachers' very carefully selected foods and drinks hint at an over-refined lifestyle far removed and alienated from natural nourishment. Except for the traditonal meal in the "Old New England" fashion (p. 264) food and eating has often degenerated to the rationally reflected intake of minerals, vitamins and calories (p. 34 f.). Eating is somehow a strained, joyless and – to Jordan – a boring affair (p. 184). Nevertheless, one of Delaney's happiest moments in those months is his shopping spree with Kyra to provide the food for their Thanksgiving dinner. He derives great satisfaction from loading their shopping cart "high with bright irresistible packages, things they needed, thing's they had run out of, things they might need or never need. Here it was, cornucopian, superabundant, all the fruits of the earth gathered and packaged and displayed for their benefit, for them and them alone" (p. 247). Buying things and food in great style and spending money without asking seems to be a psychological necessity to Americans. And as in the case of Delaney and Kyra it is also a therapy to dispel frustration and marriage strife. "That was the American way. Buy something. Feel good" (p. 149). In stark contrast Cándido and América eat left-over food sampled from restaurant trash cans, and they steal food under great scruples in order to survive. In their greatest misery Cándido kills Kyra's cat to provide his wife and the mother of his daughter with some nourishment.

7.7 Social Criticism – John Steinbeck

The idea for *The Tortilla Curtain* entered Boyle's mind when he came to see the Hispanic migrants in California as Steinbeck's "Okies of our time" (J. Steinbeck, *The Grapes of Wrath*, see box on p. 90). With the motto and epigraph taken from Steinbeck's novel, Boyle sets the urgent tone for his text. He makes us look upon human misery on the lowest possible level: there is no proper food, no proper shelter, no work, no health care; the characters' life is insecure, unprotected, devoid of basic rights, they are looked upon with suspicion and contempt even chased away from gathering places, they are the new "invisible" people (p. 197). This adjective is clearly a reference to Ralph Ellison's novel *Invisible Man* (1952) in which a young nameless black narrator grows up in a racialist world realizing that black skin in American society makes one "invisible" to white eyes. The Mexican illegal day laborers and maids go about unrecognized and unacknowledged in American society, unless they can be used as cheap labor.

All this is set in one of the world's richest countries, in one of the wealthiest U.S. states and in the wealthy community of Topanga. Thus the blatant contrast between the two human conditions raises questions of social justice, of social responsibility, and of society's moral obligation to its weakest members. Boyle feels that today as in Steinbeck's time something is brewing up, if the social imbalance and injustice remain unchanged. Moreover, he fears that overpopulation and mass immigration of various ethnic groups into California will cause uprisings and uncontrollable racism. This will put the coherence of society to a test (see Appendix 4: "Interview with T.C. Boyle"). Boyle maintains that many western societies (England, France, Germany) face the same dilemma. Closing the borders, pushing the hungry people out onto the fringes of society, fencing and walling yourself in is no answer in population conflicts.

John Steinbeck, *The Grapes of Wrath* (1939)

This famous novel tells the story of the Joad family's battle with starvation and economic desperation. Driven from their land in Oklahoma because of the drought and soil erosion they move to California hoping to make their living in what they imagine is a land of plenty. They are exploited and worn out as fruit-pickers, they are harassed by the police, they are involved in strike violence and revenge killing. They flee, lead a life of exhaustion and starvation. The eldest daughter of the family, Rose of Sharon, gives birth to a dead baby, and at the controversial end she nurses an anonymous starving man with her milk.
After publication *The Grapes of Wrath* was banned in many parts of the U.S.A., and in Steinbeck's home town Salinas it was burned twice. In 1939/40 a film (directed by John Ford, starring Henry Fonda) was produced which was true to the book capturing the Joads' tribulations and plight in a moving and authentic way. Steinbeck was awarded the prestigious Pulitzer Prize for this novel in 1940 and received the Nobel Prize for literature in 1962.

Preventing newcomers or migrants from getting a fair share of the resources or even suppressing them will lead to frustration, defiance and aggressive discontent. Like the coyote they will find ways – perhaps also violent ones – to partake in a given society's wealth. After the closing of the labor exchange Cándido's aggressive and revengeful outcry of protest may well stand for the dreaded revolutionary mood Boyle has sensed in California.

> "[...] the cars lined up like the ciphers of the wealth that bloomed all around him, unattainable as the moon. And what was it all about? Work, that was all. The right to work, to have a job, earn your daily bread and a roof over your head. He was a criminal for daring to want it, daring to risk everything for basic human necessities, and now even those were to be denied to him. It stank. It did. These people, these *norteamericanos*: what gave them the right to all the riches in the world? [...] They lived in their glass palaces, with their gates and fences and security systems, they left half-eaten lobsters and beefsteaks on their plates when the rest of the world was starving [...]. Where was the justice in that?" (p. 200)

Worked up like this Cándido is almost ready to strike back and take what he needs in an unlawful act. He fails, he is not – yet? – aggressive and determined enough for this. On the contrary, in spite of his wrath he has preserved the ethos of humanism. When he sees a white face and a white hand emerging from the swirling water, he reaches down and takes hold of it (p. 355).

7.8 Naturalism – Determinism – Social Darwinism

The "naturalist" Delaney has a biological and Darwinian view of man seeing him as just one species among others in a "grand scheme of things, drinking from the same fount as the redtailed hawk, the mule deer, the centipede and the scorpion too" (p. 78). In the fields of philosophy and literary theory this school of thought which contends that mankind is subject to the same laws as the rest of the organic and inorganic universe has come to be known as **"naturalism"**. "Men are like the *other* animals; like amoebas and the predators of the jungle" (Perry D. Westbrook, *Free Will and Determinism in American Literature*, p.115).

Men's lives and the history of their society follow firmly determined all-encompassing rules, leaving no room for something like the free will of the individual **(determinism)**. Natural determinism strongly influenced American writers such as Jack London (*The Call of the Wild*), or Theodore Dreiser (*An American Tragedy*) or William Faulkner (*Light in August*; see the names, p. 94). In the downward paths of the two Mexican underdogs, in the Eastern Liberal's road to racism and in Arroyo Blanco community's evolving xenophobia the individual's free will is shut out; instincts and social dynamics determine man's behavior. In this way we may be justified in seeing T.C. Boyle's *The Tortilla Curtain* as a novel in the American literary tradition of natural determinism.

As further proof we find a striking reference to the parable of the "squid and the lobster" told by Theodore Dreiser in his novel *The Financier*. There the boy Cowperwood watches a battle to the death between a squid and a lobster in a tank in a fish-store window. The lobster finally wins and devours the squid, because it is quicker and strategically cleverer, i.e. better endowed by nature for the fight for survival. Delaney, in comparison, once kept two scorpions in a jar and fed them with spiders. "Though one was half again as large as the other, they seemed to coexist peacefully enough until I went away for a week and returned to see the larger drinking up the vital juices of the smaller" (p. 78). The lessons of both parables are overtly **Darwinian** and refer to **the survival of the fittest**. The lobster and the stronger scorpion do not make themselves fitter. They benefit from a natural development and they use their advantages over their preys not by choice or free will but by necessity and law of nature: lobsters prey on squids, strong scorpions prey on

weak scorpions, and "strong men will devour weak men. That is the scheme of things; that is the summary of the law" (Perry D. Westbrook, p. 152).
Boyle transposes the Darwinian idea to a social level when he likens human migration to the competitive fight of animals for territory. "Obviously as a species, we move like any other animal from one area to another regardless of borders or fences or what ever, to seek resources" (Tom Lappin interview). The story of ethnic conflict in *The Tortilla Curtain* indicates that such situations result in a racism demonizing a whole ethnically different group. Before racism has muted Delaney's enlightened views, he clearly sees the danger that with the rising xenophobia in society and ongoing mass immigration violent clashes will be inevitable. He reflects upon the Americans' actions directed at driving Mexicans away from their neighborhoods and asks:

> "But where were these people supposed to go? Back to Mexico? Delaney doubted it, knowing what he did about migratory animal species and how one population responded to being displaced by another. It made for war, for violence and killing, until one group had decimated the other and reestablished its claim to the prime hunting, breeding or grazing grounds. It was a sad fact, but true." (p. 193)

It is disappointing to realize that in spite of his insights (compare also his views on the unstoppable coyote in his second column, pp. 211–215) Delaney himself finally heads down that same road of racism and violence he seems to be warning us about. The novel seems to confirm the Darwinian law that in spite of social ideals and individual goodwill instincts, personal and selfish claims as well as social dynamics will pave the way for violent population clashes.
However, one has the to take the **happy, deus ex machina ending** and the novel's protagonists as a **fable** into account. The lesson of this book is to see it as an appeal and a warning not to go down the road of xenophobia to avoid the imminent danger of ethnically motivated class wars in Western societies. At the same time one can see a moral appeal to the individual to change one's behavior and modes of thought and reach out a hand towards those who are in need.

> "The central question of this and of the images of walls that appear throughout the book […] has to do with us as a species and who owns what. Do you really own your own property? Do you have a right to fence people out? Do we have an obligation to assist people who come over that border, that wall, that gate? How is it that Americans are allowed to have this incredible standard of living while others do not?" (Interview with T.C. Boyle in the Appendix, section 4, 1st question/answer).

7.9 Autobiographical Elements

T.C. Boyle who in character definitely differs from Delaney has nevertheless incorporated some features of his life into his protagonist. In his **Darwinian world view** of competing population groups and in his warning that xenophobic backlashes against "intruding" migrants will lead to violent clashes Delaney is the author's mouthpiece (pp. 193, 241). As long as the U.S.A. attracts people who are frustrated by the conditions of poverty, unemployment and limitation in their home countries, migrants just like the coyotes "keep coming [...] moving in where the living is easy. They are cunning, versatile, hungry and unstoppable" (p. 215). And Boyle himself explains: "I've always written about man as an animal species among other animals, competing for limited resources" (Tad Friend, "Rolling Boyle", in: *The New York Times*, December 9, 1990, Late Edition; see also Boyle's statement in the Appendix, p. 105).
Like Delaney, who has recently moved from New York to California, T.C. Boyle sees himself as an **Eastern transplant**. Both maintain that they have therefore a keener sense of observing things and comparing them (pp. 240 ff.; Thanksgiving Eastern and Western Style, p. 261 f.). "I'm also an outsider here and see things differently than a California native" (Jack Rightmyer).
However different in output both Delaney and T.C. Boyle are writers by profession:

> "[...] he would be [...] sitting at his desk by nine. This was the moment he lived for, the moment his day really began. Unfailingly, no matter what pressures were brought to bear on him or what emergencies arose, he allotted the next four hours to his writing – four hours during which he could let go of the world around him, his fingers grazing lightly over the keyboard, the green glow of the monitor bathing him in its hypnotic light. He took the phone off the hook, pulled the shades and crept into the womb of language." (p. 32)

Knowing that T.C. Boyle writes "methodically from 9 a.m. to 1 p.m. seven days a week" (Tad Friend), we read the above passage right if we see this also as a depiction of his own writerly habits.

7.10 Names and Intertextual References

As to the names selected for the residents of Arroyo Blanco and Kyra's customers Boyle shows a preference for non-Anglo European immigrants' names. Many of them are derived from the Jewish-German culture (see "Grouping the Characters", p. 56). The names of Cherrystone, Doris Obst, Paulyman, Bill Vogel, Greutert, Matzoob, Mike Bender etc. and also the French Jardine are to demonstrate that it is a former but fairly **recent immigrant generation who want to see current immigrants denied entry into the U.S.A.** – a pattern that has recurred all through American immigration history.

In some subtle ways Boyle manifests his pleasure in writing. For example in police reports about the frequent accidents along the road of Topanga Canyon, i.e. along **Topanga Canyon Boulevard** and the novel's main place of action, we are surprised to find the name of the road abbreviated as **TCB**, the author's initials.
Names – people's names and place names – seem to be one of Boyle's favorite fields for allusion and irony. In the field of "water" Boyle seems especially imaginative:

- **Arroyo Blanco** = white creek; some people might remember Clinton's "Whitewater" affair which was linked up with real estate business and a scandalous housing development in Arkansas.
- **Mossbach(er)** implies a creek flowing through a "Moos"; (see also "Meaningful names", p. 54).
- Boyle is born in **Peekskill** = Peek's creek, which makes an appearance in his autobiographical novel *World's End*.
- **Teófilo Aguadulce** = Gottlieb Süß-/Sanftwasser; what a name for an adulterer!
- **Orbalina** (who also appears in the short story *Big Game*, 1994, as a maid) lives in an apartment in **Pacoima** (p. 271) meaning 'rushing water'.

Besides Orbalina there is also **Mike Bender** peopling both the short story *Big Game* and *The Tortilla Curtain*. Mike Bender, Kyra's employer, is not allowed to make an appearance in *The Tortilla Curtain*; we only know him from Kyra's reflections. In *Big Game* he is the protagonist, an extremely rich estate agent presented in full detail: Mike Bender, REALITY, 15125 Ventura Boulevard, Encino, Ca. Boyle eagerly professes that his work is full of intertextual linkings by means of names. "There are innumerable sly intertextual references throughout the work. Why? Because they are great good fun" (TCB Internet Forum), thus ruling out all postmodern antics.
A hint that is obviously no fun at all is given in the novel's title. It alludes to John Steinbeck's short novel *Tortilla Flat* (1935) which describes the lives of a group of Mexican-Americans in Monterey showing "man's proven capacity for greatness and spirit" (Steinbeck in his Nobel Prize Speech 1962). Thus Cándido's gesture at the end of *The Tortilla Curtain* reveals exactly what Steinbeck believed to be any writer's mission.
An ominous intertextual reference is to be seen in the fact that Boyle calls the evil spirit of his novel **José Navidad**. Joe Christmas is a major character in William Faulkner's novel *Light in August* (1932). In great detail its narration depicts Joe's dramatic life in which he becomes the murderer of his love and is finally killed by the National Guard.
Boyle's reference to Ralph Ellison's *Invisible Man* is also to be seen as a relevant intertextual reference drawing parallels between two historic situations

of ethnic conflict (see also p. 62). The Mexicans have taken the place of the 'Blacks' as society's most discriminated group.
As already mentioned (see p. 91) Delaney's experiment with the two scorpions alludes to Theodore Dreiser's parable of "the squid and the lobster" in *The Financier* underlining Boyle's and Delaney's Darwinian outlook. Ending again on a somewhat more amusing note we should wonder why on earth Boyle gave Kyra's pets the names of the English poets Osbert, Sacheverell and Edith Sitwell (see p. 54).

7.11 The Open Ending

When Delaney's racist fury rages highest and he is about to let loose his piled-up aggression against his victim, nature bursts with torrential floods and mountainous mudslides that drag everything and everybody off and away. All seems to be set for a tragic ending with the ruin of the protagonists. Against the readers' expectations Boyle surprises us with a "deus ex machina". In a sudden twist América and Cándido get stranded on the roof of the post office and in a melodramatic, but nevertheless powerful and hopeful image Cándido grasps the hand of his devilish enemy. It is the very man that Delaney has persecuted who saves his life in the end. Boyle maintains that the last line of the novel expresses his basic message. In an interview translated into German he explains it like this: „Wenn du an der letzten Zeile angelangt bist, weißt du, dass wir alle Menschen sind, du kannst diese Menschen nicht dämonisieren" (Uli Hufen, popsprite). We wonder if Delaney will have learned that powerful lesson of humanism. What do you think?

> "I have always found the ending of *The Tortilla Curtain* to be positive in an admittedly complex way – the reaching out by one to save the other in the middle of devastation (one that bears a striking resemblance to the Tsunami) showing that we know how to come together. And it's left to the reader to decide, why we are not cohesive as a world of humans, unless there are tragedies pulling us together." (Kaytie, in the TCB Forum, Internet)

V Appendix

1. Structure in Overview: Alternating Chapters and Temporal Order

Part One: Arroyo Blanco

Ch.	Persp.	Action	Time
(1)	D	**Delaney** injures a Mexican pedestrian.	a day at the end of June
(2)	C A	**Cándido** is run over by an American; he recovers only slowly; **América** goes up to the labor exchange.	on the same day three consecutive days 4th **day** in the morning
(3)	D	**Delaney** is having breakfast with wife and son; a coyote grabs Sacheverell; **Delaney** attends the meeting about the gate and makes a fool of himself.	4th **day** in the morning in the evening
(4)	A C	**América** again goes to the labor exchange; Jack Jr. devastates their camp.	5th **day**
(5)	D K	After the community meeting **Delaney** comes across Jack Jr.; "therapeutic sex"; **Kyra's** job; **Delaney** writes his article.	4th **day:** late in the evening 5th **day**
(6)	A C	**América** gets work with Jim Shirley; Cándido encounters José Navidad; **América** returns very late.	8th **day**
(7)	D	**Delaney** shops for a few urgent things; Discussion with Jack Sr.; Delaney encounters Cándido on the parking lot. **Delaney** meets José Navidad on his hike; he goes back to find his car stolen.	8th **day** in the early evening 9th **day** morning
(8)	C A	Both **Cándido and América** go up to the labor exchange; América is again hired by Jim Shirley; in the evening she returns to their camp, but does not find Cándido. She is raped by José Navidad.	9th **day morning**

D = Delaney K = Kyra C = Cándido A = América

Part Two: El Tenksgeevee

Ch.	Persp.	Action	Time
(1)	D K	**Delaney** buys a new Acura car, has lunch with Kyra; **Kyra** checks Al Lopez and the new fence; she meets Cándido.	**9th day** noon afternoon
(2)	C A	Al Lopez hires **Cándido** after 12 o'clock; he works late; learns about "the robbery". Cándido has regular work with Al Lopez; América must stay in the camp; Cándido is dismissed by Al Lopez; at his barbecue he gets drunk heavily.	**9th day** noon late at night **3 weeks** **31st day:** **end of July**
(3)	D	**Delaney's** refined barbecue with Kyra; a coyote climbs over the new fence; it grabs Osbert; flashback: Delaney joins his neighbors who want to build a wall.	a Sunday in **mid-August**
(4)	C A	**Cándido** finds work for 5 days; closure of the labor exchange; **Cándido and América** walk to Canoga Park to find an apartment; day-long walk.	**end of August** **"Canoga Park" day** early September
(5)	D	The Coyote – **Delaney's** monthly column	
(6)	K – D	Kyra checks the Da Roses' house and is confronted by José Navidad.	late summer afternoon
(7)	C A	**Cándido** is beaten up and robbed; they walk back to their camp.	**"Canoga Park" day**
(8)	D	Delaney and Kyra go shopping together;	**Thanksgiving Day**
	A C	**América** falls into depression and apathy; **Cándido** is hired twice; Cándido goes shopping and is given a turkey; América cheers up; **the fire gets out of control.**	time after **"Canoga Park" day** **Thanksgiving Day** afternoon

Part Three: Socorro

Ch.	Persp.	Action	Time
(1)	D – K	Cocktail party interrupted by brush fire, **Delaney and Kyra** evacuate their home.	**Thanksgiving Day** 4 o'clock
(2)	C – A	**Cándido and América** escape from the fire in a shed near the wall; América goes into labor.	**Thanksgiving Day** late at night
(3)	D	**Delaney and Kyra** watch the fire; José Navidad is arrested, spits in Delaney's face; in the morning the fire is contained and people can return to their houses.	**Thanksgiving Day** late in the evening **Friday**
(4)	C	**América** gives birth to Socorro late at night; **Cándido** builds a hut.	**Thanksgiving Day** **Friday morning**
(5)	K – D	**Kyra** visits the destroyed Da Ros place. The couple take a stroll: graffiti on the wall. The rainy season starts.	**Sunday** November – December
(6)	C	**Cándido** does not get any work; on his way home his walk is blocked by "his" crazy American.	November – December some days **before Christmas**
(7)	D K	**Delaney** blocks the way of "his" Mexican but fails to have him arrested; he follows the Mexican's footprints to Arroyo Blanco; Delaney follows the smell of smoke; Kyra crosses "the border".	shortly before **Christmas** **in the late evening**
(8)	A	**Cándido** is back at their new shelter; suddenly "his" crazy American jumps in and threatens them with a gun;	**the same day at night**
	D	**Delaney** finds the hut and jumps in with his gun in his hand.	
	C – D C	**Cándido, América and Delaney** – all three are swept away by a mudslide; **Cándido** rescues **Delaney**.	**at night**

2. Political Correctness – Liberalism – Humanism

What is "political correctness" in the U.S.A.?

Political correctnes is a term to denote a set of liberal attitudes about education and society, and the language associated with them. To be politically correct is to be sensitive to unconscious racism and sexism and to display environmental awareness. This sensitivity is to be expressed in a non-discriminatory language towards all social and ethnic groups and individuals. However, attempts at enforcing PC speech codes (e. g. 'people of color' instead of 'colored people', 'differently abled' instead of 'disabled') have been ridiculed and criticized as a form of thought police.

What is a "liberal" in the U.S.A.?

The most common contemporary U.S. use of the term *liberal* is somewhat at variance from the use of the term in the rest of the world and so also from the idea of political liberalism in Germany. Americans usually define liberals as those who support the use of government power to promote equality, but generally not to promote order. U.S. liberals also are more likely to openly support the legitimacy of government with regard to social intervention than are conservatives.
The following views could be considered typical of American liberalism today:

- Support for government social programs such as welfare, medical care, unemployment benefits, and retirement programs
- Support for public education
- Support for trade unions – right of labor to organize
- Regulation of business – against child labor, monopolistic practices, etc.
- Support for civil rights (examples):
  - Oppose discrimination based on gender, race, age, religion, sexual orientation, or disability
  - Support for rights of women and minorities, particularly racial and religious minorities, the disabled, and homosexuals
  - Some further support such programs and multilingual education
  - Support for abortion rights
- Support for strong environmental regulations
- Support for minimum wage requirements
- Opposition to the death penalty
- Support for gun controls

What is a "humanist" in the U.S.A.?

Humanism: the idea that every human being has worth and dignity.

"Humanism is a democratic and ethical life stance which affirms that human beings have the right and responsibility to give meaning and shape to their own lives. It stands for the building of a more humane society through an ethics based on human and other natural values in a spirit of reason and free inquiry through human capabilities. It is not theistic, and it does not accept supernatural views of reality."

At its last meeting (Mexico City, November, 1996) the Board of the International Humanist and Ethical Union approved this "minimum statement" of Humanism.

Humanist beliefs and practices:

- Humanists value knowledge based on reason and hard evidence rather than on faith.
- Being secular Humanists, they reject the concept of a personal God, and regard humans as supreme. From this belief naturally follows:
  - "The preciousness and dignity of the individual person is a central humanist value."
  - a rejection of a created universe in favor of the theory of evolution
  - a rejection of divinely inspired ethical and moral codes in favor of codes derived by reason from the human condition
  - the belief that full responsibility for the future of the world, its political systems, its ecology, etc. rests with humans. There is no God in heaven to intervene.
  - They accept democracy and reject all systems that are dangerous to individual freedom.
  - They value freedom of inquiry, expression and action.
  - They are energetic supporters of the separation of church and state.
  - They have liberal beliefs about controversial ethical topics, like abortion or homosexuality.

3. Nativism in the U.S.A.

In the middle of the 19th century immigration numbers started to rise sharply due to the famine in Ireland, political suppression and economic depression in Europe. As early as the 1840s groups of activists opposing the onsetting immigration wave founded a secret society, the so-called "Know-Nothing Party" (its members were sworn to respond "I know nothing" when asked about the party). Although this party soon faded away there was considerable hostility in the 1860s and 1870s against Irish, Catholic and Chinese immigrants ."NO IRISH NEED APPLY" read some of the adverts for jobs and there were anti-Chinese riots in California. When mass immigration started in the 1880s (especially from Eastern, South Eastern and Southern Europe) the

xenophobic sentiment among the **native-born** Americans deepened. The **nativists** believed that the influx of immigrants was far too great, and they spread the fears that these people would steal the jobs of the native-born Americans.
Moreover, they complained that immigration would lead to the exploitation of the American workers, as the newly arrived immigrants were willing to work for low wages, thus creating intolerable working conditions. Many of the new immigrants were Catholic or Jewish, most of them did not speak English, and their customs differed strongly from the Anglo-Protestant society of the U.S.A. In the ethnic neighborhoods of many American cities – e. g. in the " little Germanies", "little Italies", or the quarters inhabited by Easter European Jews – the immigrants stayed together and stuck to their particular habits and customs (in today's Germany we would speak of 'Parallelgesellschaften'). In Nativists' eyes this situation was proof that the new immigrants failed to adapt to their new lives as Americans.
Social history shows that the economic fears in the expanding American economy were unfounded as jobs were abundant and that in a three-generation pattern most immigrants became assimilated Americans. In a nation of immigrants the process of acculturation was and still is not a one-way street. American culture was influenced, changed, enriched by elements of immigrants' cultures. Music, theater, literature, cuisine, restaurants, festivals became more varied and colorful broadening the cultural life of America. Immigrant artists, scientists, and intellectuals left their distinctive marks contributing richly to American culture.
With masses seeking entry into the U.S.A. in the decades between 1880 – 1920 and 1970 – 2000 it would be blue-eyed to hold the view of unrestricted access to the country. The history of American immigration laws illustrates the endeavors to regulate the influx in a way that takes both sides into account, i.e. responding generously to those who want to become Americans and avoiding undue strain on American communities and native-born citizens.
The influx of Asians and Hispanics in the last three decades leading to far-reaching change in the ethnic make-up of American society (see pp. 12 ff.) has renewed fears of the loss of the centers of American culture (the English language; basic values) and also revived nativist sentiments. The Californian Proposition 187 (see p. 15) can be taken at least partly as proof for the rise of nativism.

4. *From:* An Interview with T.C. Boyle

(Penguin Reading Guides: *The Tortilla Curtain*)

What is the significance of the title of the book?

The title comes from a common phrase for the Mexican border, **The Tortilla Curtain**, and I envision it in this way. We have the Iron Curtain, which as an image is impenetrable. You picture this wall across Eastern Europe. Then we have the Bamboo Curtain with regard to China. As I see it, that isn't quite as impenetrable as an iron curtain. It shatters easily and has gaps in it. It's not uniform. And now we have **The Tortilla Curtain**, which is the opposite of impregnable. It's three strips of barbed wire with some limp tortillas hanging on it. The central question of this, and of the images of walls that appear throughout the book – the walls, the gates, walling people out, what do you wall in, all of that – has to do with us as a species and who owns what. Do you really own your own property? Do you have a right to fence people out? Do we have an obligation to assist people who come over that border, that wall, that gate? How is it that Americans are allowed to have this incredible standard of living while others do not? All of these questions, I think, are wrapped up in my view of our debate over immigration.

What is your view on immigration?

I feel that, on the one hand, we do have a right to be a sovereign nation and to protect our borders. Illegal immigration makes a mockery of legal immigration, and no other country in the world allows this sort of thing to happen. On the other hand, what I object to even more than that is this kind of demonizing of a whole race and class of people, as in considering all Mexicans, all Guatemalans, all Salvadorans to be bad because they're invading our country as impoverished and ignorant individuals. The final gesture of the book, I think, shows you that we are one species and we do have to understand and appreciate that fact despite ethnic and national differences. But it's a small gesture because I think that it's a very, very complex issue that people have to work towards answering.

[...]

The book is essentially set in your own backyard. Did this prompt you to write it? Did the proposal and passing of Proposition 187 (a bill passed in California that denies certain social benefits to illegal immigrants) factor in?

The book was somewhat misunderstood because it came out after the 187 vote, and people attacked the book or enjoyed it based on their own perspective. The book was actually conceived and written prior to Proposition 187's even being drafted, and I think it came from the fact that I lived in Los Angeles for sixteen years. Reading about immigration in the newspaper every day and talking to people at parties like the ones that Delaney and Kyra give, I began to get a sense of something brewing that was akin to what happened here in Steinbeck's day, but had the added element that the Okies of today are not American citizens and they're of a different race.

Do you see *The Tortilla Curtain* as a political novel?

I think obviously people will want to talk about 187, and the campaign to draft a national bill like 187, but this book isn't a political novel in the sense that it takes a position and is meant to have people agree or disagree with that position. It's political in a different sense. I don't think political novels work because they have "an ax to grind." If you have "an ax to grind," then you have to sacrifice aesthetics and the discovery of the book in order to make your point or to make people join your party or to see your point of view. I write a book like **The Tortilla Curtain** from having lived here and picked up on everything going on that finally resulted in 187, and from trying to sort out my own feelings. I don't have a position when I begin a book, any book. I write in order to put some hypothetical elements together and see what will happen. I don't know what's going to happen even chapter by chapter, and I don't know what's going to happen at the end of the book. That's a process of discovery, which is why I write novels rather than, let's say, a polemic, to discover how I feel about the issues, but particularly about this issue.

Critics and readers on both sides of the immigration issue had mixed reactions to *The Tortilla Curtain*. Why do you think the book generated so much controversy?

I'm not presenting any answers, and I think that's why the book was very controversial. People want a polemic. They want to raise their fist in the air and say, "Yes, you're on our side." Well, I'm not on your side. I am presenting a fable, a fiction, so that you can judge for yourself. A lot of people simply read the book and flew off the handle because it either accords with what they want it to or it doesn't. People want things to be very clear-cut. Here's the issue and here's how I stand on it. But I think it's much more complex. I think it has to do with biology. You may notice that Delaney is a nature writer. Well, nature writers are generally very liberal, even radically liberal on all issues except one – the issue of immigration, on which they are more reactionary than anyone. The reason for this is they argue that there are six billion people on the planet now, and who is the enemy of the environment? Who is the enemy of clean air, clean water, all the dwindling animal species? Well, it's us. Us, human beings. Our species. And this is an element of the book which is very important and has been overlooked. There is this population pressure on the world in all the industrial nations, not simply the United States. England, Germany, and France all have huge influxes of immigrants, and I'm wondering, what does this mean and how are people going to deal with it? I think ultimately, as you see in **The Tortilla Curtain**, it may simply exacerbate racist tendencies.

What research did you do to prepare for the writing of *The Tortilla Curtain*?

It may sound silly, but I've always felt an affection for Mexico and Mexican culture. I grew up in New York, as you may know, and the language I studied from eighth grade on was Spanish. In fact, the only language I can speak besides English is Spanish. I've always been attracted to the culture, and even before I moved to California I had traveled in Mexico and Central America. When I decided to write this book, I knew that I had to see one thing only. And that was the fence at the border. So I went back to Tijuana, where I hadn't been for some years, and spent the day there. I talked to people. I walked along the fence. I saw people waiting to climb over the fence with little plastic bags with everything they owned in them. I saw the border guards eyeing me suspiciously from the other side. I saw the huge fence the U.S. is building out into the water, and so on, just to get a feel for that again and see what it's like. And it's a real war zone, it's a real disaster, Tijuana, let me tell you.

The search for the American dream is a theme that resounds throughout *The Tortilla Curtain*. Do you think there is such a thing as the American dream?

I've addressed this throughout all of my work, our material obsession, all the stuff I've written about eating and how much we have and the surfeit of things; my story "Filthy with Things," for instance. What is the American dream? Well, the American dream is, "you pull yourself up by your bootstraps, you make it, you have a house, you live in the suburbs, and you drive a new car." What is that? That is a material dream. If you have nothing, then you have material dreams. Presumably, if you have an education and you have enough to eat, then you can have aesthetic dreams or humanistic dreams. Easy for me to say. I have every material thing I could want. I didn't become a writer to make money. I became a writer because that is my obsession and that's how I view the world. As a novelist, my job is to try to inhabit people of any culture, to be a person of another sex, or another race, or another ethnic group. I think it helps me to understand them, and it helps the reader to understand them, too.

5. Illegal Aliens in Germany

"You will find them everywhere: on building sites, in restaurants, in private homes as maids or nurses. They constitute an important economic factor, but officially they are non-existent – illegal migrants without any legimitation. And the consequences: they toil from dawn to dusk for minimal wages, they are exploited by employers, they pay exorbitant rent for underhand accommodation, they are not entitled to medicare – and they live in constant fear of being picked up by public officials and turned out of the country" (Die *Rheinpfalz*, Christmas 2004).

Turned out of which country? Sounds American. No, it's Germany. The official report on migration in Germany counts about 100,000 apprehensions of illegal immigrants for the year 2003. In most cases these are so-called "Asylanten" without any valid permit to stay in the country. As to the number of illegal immigrants in Germany churches and human rights organizations estimate that there are about **one million illegal immigrants living in Germany**.

To them, as to Cándido and América, one of the most troubling grievances is what to do in case of illness. In Germany according to its Ausländergesetz anybody helping or caring for illegal migrants commits the offence of "Beihilfe". Nevertheless, there are doctors and organizations like "Malteser Migranten Medizin" that assist illegal migrants and see to it that they are provided with efficient medical treatment although they are not insured and often cannot pay the bills.

One of the doctors in Berlin is Mrs. Franz, who cares for pregnant women. She sees to it that pregnant women are prepared well for giving birth to their babies and that they find clinics which deliver the babies without asking too many questions. In 2004 Mrs. Franz assisted 84 women to have their babies in this way. Most of the expenses are paid for from donations, but many migrants contribute to it with at least a small amount of money. Mrs. Franz hopes that one day everybody in the country – no matter what status – will be entitled to fundamental basic humanitarian rights including the right to basic medicare.

6. Why Read *The Tortilla Curtain* this side of the Atlantic?

T.C. Boyle's View

The social microcosm of the "dual world" of *The Tortilla Curtain* is full of misery on the Mexican side and contempt and xenophobia on the American side. I am extremely grateful to T.C. Boyle for sending me this short statement on why, in his opinion, German and other European high school students should be confronted with this bitter, but moving and heart-wrenching American story.

K.E. Schuhmacher

Dear Karl:

Here is a brief statement for you re. The Tortilla Curtain.

I do believe that The Tortilla Curtain remains a powerful and viable book which speaks to any number of cultures, particularly those in what we have termed the First World. Such cultures--European, American, Japanese, etc.--have been more fortunate than others and lay claim to a disproportionate allowance of the world's resources. It is only to be expected that people from the Third World will emigrate to those countries in order to share in the resources. We are an animal species, no different in many respects from the coyotes of The Tortilla Curtain, creatures that thrive because they must. As the resources of the world shrink drastically (see my 2000 novel A Friend of the Earth, as well as Jared Diamond's recent Collapse, Bill McKibben's The End of Nature, Laurie Garret's The Coming Plague and other environmental texts), we can expect to see traditional national identities in melt-down. What will come of this is up to us and to our attitudes toward one another. The Tortilla Curtain, published ten years ago this coming fall, speaks to these issues in what I hope is a compelling way. If it is provocative, if it makes you angry or sad, then it is doing its job as literature--it is meant to be provocative, meant to stir thought and debate. But because it is a novel --a work of art--it does not presume to make pronouncements or to impose a meaning or a solution: all this is for the reader to discover on his or her own.

T.C. Boyle
Santa Barbara, CA
April 2005

7. Maps

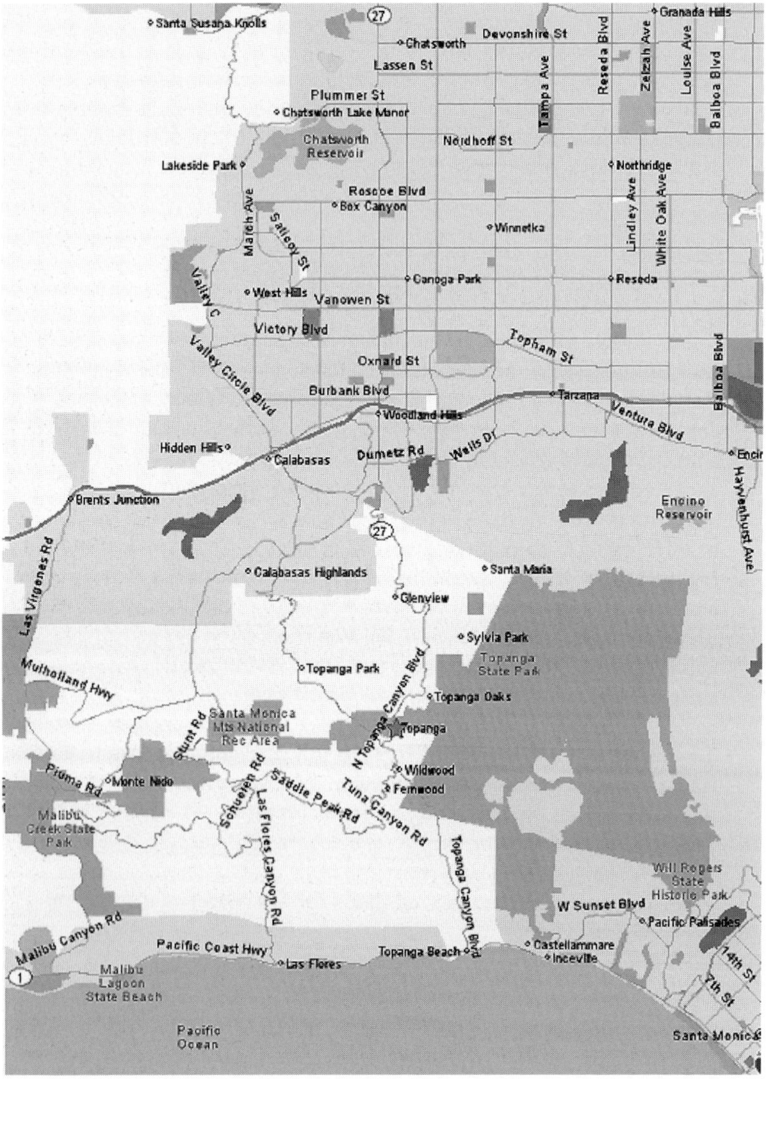
Santa Susana Knolls
Chatsworth
Devonshire St
Granada Hills
Lassen St
Reseda Blvd
Zelzah Ave
Louise Ave
Balboa Blvd
Tampa Ave
Plummer St
Chatsworth Lake Manor
Chatsworth Reservoir
Nordhoff St
Lakeside Park
Northridge
Roscoe Blvd
Box Canyon
Marsh Ave
Saticoy St
Winnetka
Lindley Ave
White Oak Ave
Canoga Park
Reseda
West Hills
Vanowen St
Valley C
Victory Blvd
Topham St
Valley Circle Blvd
Oxnard St
Burbank Blvd
Tarzana
Woodland Hills
Ventura Blvd
Hidden Hills
Calabasas
Dumetz Rd
Wells Dr
Encino
Brents Junction
Hayvenhurst Ave
Encino Reservoir
Las Virgenes Rd
Calabasas Highlands
Santa Maria
Glenview
Sylvia Park
Topanga State Park
Mulholland Hwy
Topanga Park
Topanga Canyon Blvd
Topanga Oaks
Stunt Rd
Santa Monica Mts National Rec Area
N Topanga
Topanga
Piuma Rd
Monte Nido
Schueren Rd
Saddle Peak Rd
Wildwood
Fernwood
Tuna Canyon Rd
Las Flores Canyon Rd
Malibu Creek State Park
Will Rogers State Historic Park
W Sunset Blvd
Pacific Palisades
Malibu Canyon Rd
Pacific Coast Hwy
Las Flores
Topanga Beach
Castellammare
Inceville
14th St
7th St
Malibu Lagoon State Beach
Pacific Ocean
Santa Monica
27
1

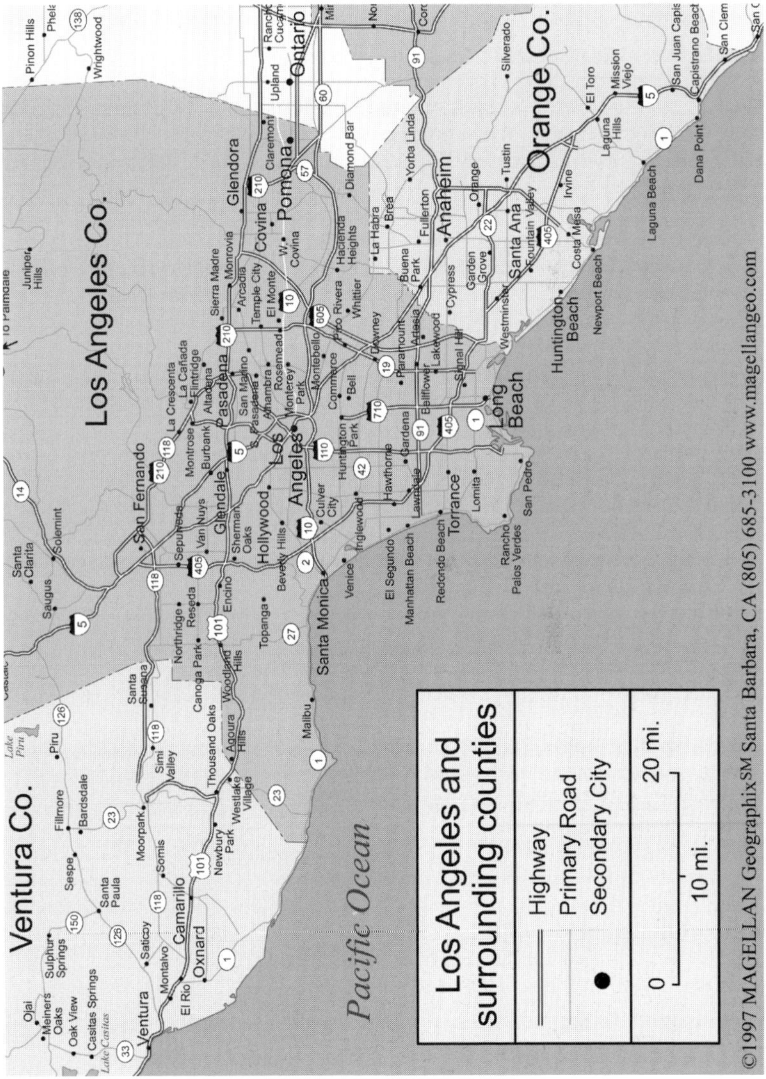
Los Angeles and surrounding counties
Highway
Primary Road
Secondary City
0
10 mi.
20 mi.
Ventura Co.
Los Angeles Co.
Orange Co.
Pacific Ocean
Ventura
Oxnard
Camarillo
Thousand Oaks
Simi Valley
Malibu
Santa Monica
San Fernando
Glendale
Pasadena
Los Angeles
Hollywood
Torrance
Long Beach
Pomona
Ontario
Covina
Glendora
Anaheim
Santa Ana
Huntington Beach
Newport Beach
Laguna Beach
Dana Point
San Juan Capistrano
Irvine
Costa Mesa
Fullerton
Orange
©1997 MAGELLAN GeographixSM Santa Barbara, CA (805) 685-3100 www.magellangeo.com

8. Bibliography

Barnes and Noble, Meet the Writer: T.C. Boyle: www.BarnesandNoble.com
Birnbaum, Robert, "Robert Birnbaum Talks with the Author of *Drop City*", 2003 (Internet).
Blakely, Edward. J. / Snyder, Mary Gail, *Fortress America. Gated Communities in The United States,* Washington 1999.
Boyle, T. C., "This Monkey, My Back. Autobiographical Essay", in: Frank Conroy, ed., *The Eleventh Draft*, New York: HarperCollins, 1999.
Ciotto, Paul, "The Hemingway of the Hudson", in: *Hudson Valley Magazine*, December 1987, pp. 49–51.
Crawford, James, "Cycles of Nativism in U.S. History", National Immigration Forum, 2001: www.immigrationforum.org
Eggers, David, "A Contemporary Fable about Immigration", in: *San Francisco Chronicle*, September 10, 1995.
Francis, Sam, "Immigration vs. 'Anglo-Protestant' America", in: *Sam Francis Archive*, February, 26, 2004 (Internet).
Freese, Peter, "T. Coraghessan Boyle's *The Tortilla Curtain*: A Case Study in the Genesis of Xenophobia", in: Heinz Antor / Klaus Stiersdorfer, eds., *English Literatures in International Contexts*, Heidelberg: Winter, 2000, pp. 221–243.
Friedland, Jared, "Black Humor, Leaning toward the Absurd. An Interview with Author T.C. Boyle", *Education Update Online*, May 2004.
Friend, Tad, "Rolling Boyle", in: *The New York Times*, December 9, 1990, Sunday Late Edition.
Hufen, Uli, "Immigration, Politik und die Kunst, das zu tun, was keiner erwartet", Interview mit T.C. Boyle (popsprite/Internet).
Hume, Kathryn, *American Dream – American Nightmare. Fiction since 1960*, Urbana: University of Illinois Press, 2002.
Lappin, Tom, "Text Mex", in: *The Scotsman*, November 10, 1995.
Nachman, Barbara, "Hometown Rebel", in: *The Journal News* (New York), November 12, 1998.
Penguin Reading Guides, *The Tortilla Curtain* by T.C. Boyle (Internet; with appraisal, study questions and an interview with T.C. Boyle).
Rightmeyer, Jack, "T.C. Boyle Says Books Saved His Life", in: *The Daily Gazette*, Albany, N.Y., February 23, 2003.
Schröder, Markus, *Nice Guys Finish Last: Sozialkritik in den Romanen T. Coraghessan Boyles*, Essen: Die Blaue Eule, 1997.
Spencer, Scott, "The Pilgrim of Topanga Creek", in: *The New York Times*, September 3, 1995, Late Edition.
St. James Encyclopedia of Popular Culture, St. James Press 1999.
Valenzuela, Abel, "Working on the Margins: Immigrant Day Labor", The Center for Cooperative Immgration Studies, San Diego: University of California, Working Paper No. 22, May, 2000.
Weber, Bruce, "Novel Appeal", in: *The New York Times Magazine*, March 19, 1989.
Westbrook, Perry D., *Free Will and Determinism in American Literature*, Cranbury, N.J.: Associated University Presses, 1979.

VI Model Questions and Tasks

A. Questions and Answers

Comprehension

1. Write a chronology of the main events of the novel.

action in flashbacks
(years computed)

1960s and 1970s	Cándido's childhood and youth in Tepotzlán.
1980	Cándido marries Resurreción; América, aged 4, is one of the flower girls at the wedding.
1980–1987	Cándido goes north to the U.S.A. for some months every year leaving his wife behind in Tepotzlán.
1987	His wife is made pregnant by another man and leaves Cándido.
1992	Cándido meets América (16 years old) again, falls in love with her and they leave for the U.S.A. in spring 1993.
June 1993	Cándido and América try to find work in Topanga; they camp out in Topanga Canyon.

action proper
from June 1993 to December 1993

Part One

end of June	Accident: Delaney hits Cándido with his car.
nine days	Cándido's slow recovery from his injuries; América finds a work for two days with Jim Shirley; Cándido is employed by Al Lopez; América is raped; Delaney's and Kyra's work and daily life; a coyote grabs a dog; home owners vote for the erection of a gate; car theft.

Part Two

three weeks in July	Delaney buys a new car; Cándido gets work with Al Lopez; América is confined to the camp; Cándido is fired.
a Sunday mid-August	Delaney's and Kyra's barbecue; a coyote grabs and kills Osbert; the residents' plans for "the wall".
end of August	Cándido finds work for five days.
early September	Cándido and América walk to Canoga Park to find an apartment there; beaten and robbed of their money, they return to their camp.
Thanksgiving Day	Delaney's and Kyra's shopping spree at Gitello's; Cándido is given a turkey and América comes out of her depression; Cándido causes a big brush fire.

Part Three

Thanksgiving Day	Delaney and Kyra have to leave Dom Flood's cocktail party because of the fire to prepare evacuation measures; they leave their home and stay at a hotel for the night.
Thursday night	Cándido and América can escape from the fire; Socorro is born.
Friday morning	Cándido builds a new shelter; the Arroyo Blanco residents can return to their homes.
late November/ December	The rainy season starts; Cándido does not get any work.
shortly before Christmas	Delaney tries to get Cándido arrested by the police; he damages his car; Delaney attacks the couple in their shelter; a sudden mudslide sweeps them all away; the miraculous rescue.

2. **Make a list of the stores and services in and around fictional Topanga. Try to detect their locations.**

- a nursery and garden center on the Coast Highway
- a gas station where Topanga Canyon Boulevard joins the Coast Highway
- a lumber yard a hundred yards up Topanga Canyon Road from the place of the accident
- The first store coming up from the lower Topanga Canyon is Li's grocery store with telephones out front (pp. 21, 112).

- The post office and the labor exchange is a bit further up where the old Canyon Road turns off left from Topanga Canyon Boulevard.
- At this central spot there is also a gas station, a second-hand clothing store, Gitello's supermarket and a little store run by the paisano from Italy.
- Kenny Grissom's Acura dealership, garage and showroom
- Jordan's elementary school
- a recycling center further up Topanga Canyon Boulevard towards Calabasas
- Mike Bender's real estate office in Woodland Hills (Kyra's office)
- a huge supermarket and the Holiday Inn Hotel in Woodland Hills

Analysis and Interpretation

3. Describe the main stages of Delaney's development from the self-proclaimed "liberal humanist" to the racist activist. Discuss the causes for this change of attitude.

Delaney's "liberal creed"

He holds the following views to be self-evident
- that immigrants are the "lifeblood of this country", that America is a nation of immigrants, and that "neither of us would be standing here if it wasn't" (p. 101);
- that Hispanic immigrants have every right, an "inalienable" (p. 185) right to gather at street corners or wherever they want to; one cannot distinguish between legal and illegal aliens once they are in the country (p. 185);
- that the Mexicans will eventually assimilate just as the Poles, Italians, Germans, Irish and Chinese did in the past (p. 102);
- that the gate is an absurdity, intimidating, exclusionary, anti-democratic (p. 41);
- that walling in their community is a relapse into medieval times (p. 189).

Delaney's road from a liberal humanist to a law-and-order racist

- Delaney suspects he has become **victim of a faked accident** to be robbed (p. 6).
- He is annoyed at **illegals camping out and polluting** rivers and trails (p. 11).
- He is greatly irritated that **so many Mexicans** are in Californian service jobs (p. 12).
- He reconsiders his liberal stand when he thinks of **crime** (p. 43).
- At night on his way home he is followed by a car and **feels frightened** (p. 64).
- He gives in to Jack Jardine to satisfy his craving for security: "I don't like the gate – but I accept it. None of us want **urban crime** up here" (p. 104).
- On one of his walks his way is blocked by José and his companion whom he suspects of camping out in the lower canyon; in the fashion of a **law and order** adherent he will see to it that the sheriff intervenes and expels them: "They didn't belong here" (p. 117).

- The **car theft** leaves behind a sense of great vulnerability in Delaney (p. 155 f.).
- When he hands over the key of his brand-new car to a Mexican attendant, he experiences a "**deep shameful stab of racist resentment** – did they all have to be Mexican?" (p. 149).
- Delaney **violently attacks** José on Thanksgiving Day (pp. 286 – 290) without having proof.
- Delaney becomes obsessed with the idea of catching the graffiti sprayers whom he presumes to be the arsonists as well; he thinks of **direct cooperation with the INS** (p. 317).
- Delaney's **hatred** turns in increased intensity against Cándido, "his" Mexican (p. 320).
- Delaney recognizes Cándido on the canyon road, and in **vigilante fashion** tries to have him arrested (p. 332 f.): "all he cared about was this Mexican, the man who'd invaded his life like some unshakeable parasite, like a disease" (p. 332).
- Delaney has earlier bought **a gun** (p. 342).
- Delaney continues his man hunt although he finds out that Jack Jr. is the graffiti sprayer; **with gun in hand** Delaney breaks into Cándido's and América's hut.

4. Delaney hits Cándido with his car, but after the first shock he more and more sees himself as the "victim". Explain his attitude.

- When Delaney does not find the injured man, he thinks of a staged accident intended to rob him.
- He is annoyed that some illegal alien dashes across the street in suicidal manner and brings his life into disorder.
- The image of the Mexican keeps haunting him, disturbing his peace of mind.
- The incident in the parking lot of the supermarket to him is another proof that this man is a nuisance repeatedly troubling other people.
- Delaney sees Cándido's face on one of the photos his surveillance cameras have taken and understands that it was this man who stole the things from their gardens and garden sheds.

5. Characterize Delaney's and Kyra's way of life. What are their aspirations?

Delaney

- The center of his life is rooted in his job as a writer; the time allotted to writing – every day from nine to one o'clock – is sacred to him; he lives for these fulfilling moments; he is strongly annoyed and irritated, if for some reason he is disturbed in his reflections and in the process of writing; in this case the day is spoiled for him.
- He is convinced that he is some kind of a seer who feels more deeply about nature than others, and he thinks it to be his duty to communicate this to others.
- His aspirations for material success have already been fulfilled; he knows that he is fortunate to have a house in that privileged spot.
- He is happy with Kyra and their life together; he is glad to have left the years of loneliness behind.
- His wish to have a baby – it would be his only child – is not fulfilled by Kyra.
- In spite of his false tone celebrating nature we should take his craving for an unpolluted and balanced environment seriously.

Kyra

- She would like to be seen as a power seller ("volume leader") with the personal touch; her personal courtesies are to set the tone for polite and friendly business relations to customers and colleagues; she wants to be regarded as a person of unending goodwill.
- She dreams of once owning a "palace" like the Da Roses' mansion; when it is destroyed her longing is find a substitute in an even bigger and greater mansion in even more extensive and rural grounds.
- She wants to acquire as much money as possible to be able to leave Mike Bender's estate business and be her own real estate boss.
- She becomes aware of the tediousness of her daily routines of listing and selling properties; her final aspiration is developing residential areas on a grand scale.

6. **Characterize Cándido's and América's aspirations for their life in the U.S.A. Describe how their American dream turns into a nightmare.**

Cándido's and América's dream

- Cándido's main aspiration is just work, "the right to work, to have a job, earn your daily bread and a roof over your head" (p. 200).
- But he is also attracted by the traditional elements of the American dream: a TV, a car, a washing machine, a vacuum cleaner (p. 29).
- From his earnings he saves the money to get an apartment; it is the starting point to be able to lead a decent life with steady work.
- He hopes that they will get their green cards eventually or that they may benefit from another amnesty and in this way will be able to leave the life in illegality (p. 199).
- Cándido wants to provide América with a life of security: "a real house in a real neighborhood with laws and respect and human dignity"(p. 27).
- América "dreams" of a "clean white lumber house" with a small yard, a garden and with some space to keep chickens (p. 29).
- Troubled by the proceeding pregnancy and Cándido's bad luck she reduces her wishes: she would be content with living in an apartment with a clean kitchen, a hot shower and a toilet.

Their dreams denied

- There is a never-ending series of bad luck: Cándido's injuries prevent him from getting work; after José's attack on América she can no longer go and seek work; Al Lopez fires Cándido when his green card worker is fit for work again; the Topanga labor exchange is closed; for lack of money Cándido and América cannot rent an apartment to start a more dignified life; when they try to rent one for just one night, Cándido's credulity costs them the little money they have: he is beaten up and robbed by a countryman; they hit rock bottom.
- Their life after this incident is one of utter misery and destitution; they live on refuse and there are ill feelings between them.
- Their life has turned into a nightmare: it is late fall, the rainy season will start any day, they still live out in the open, and soon their child will be born.
- They barely escape from the fire on Thanksgiving Day; América must climb rocks and a steep dump despite her pregnancy; she gives birth to her daughter in a hut with Cándido acting as midwife; although there is no proper hygiene and food, all seems to go well with Socorro and her mother.
- Socorro is born blind.

7. **Cándido sees his "personal" devil in Delaney.**
Study and explain the various encounters between Delaney and him from Cándido's point of view.

- The injuries inflicted on him by Delaney make Cándido suffer immensely.
- That same red-haired devil is present when he is bullied by the huge American.
- Cándido thinks that the youth who devastated their shelter is Delaney's son, another red-haired devil.
- The mad American, i.e. Delaney, blocks Cándido's way home on Topanga Canyon Road almost at the same spot where the accident happened.
- The enraged Delaney jumps into Cándido's and América's hut with gun in his hand threatening the couple and their baby.

8. **Describe the narrative technique by which the lives of the two couples are presented in the novel. Discuss the differences in the author's portrayal of the American and Mexican characters.**
Does he treat them equally fairly?

- The four major characters are presented by a third-person narrator who speaks through their minds.
- The chapters alternate in their points of view between the American and the Mexican couples.
- Quantitatively speaking, both couples are treated equally; the male characters of each couple are each given more room for the development of their stories – the female characters are less prominent and Kyra especially is not allowed to develop a full personality.
- By satirizing the behavior, views and characters of the Americans, especially of Delaney, the narrator holds them up to ridicule and evokes criticism in the reader; our sympathy is distinctly guided and directed towards the unlucky Mexicans.
- América's and Cándido's story is depicted with great sympathy and compassion; we cannot but feel pity for their constant bad luck and their unbearable situation.
- Whereas there are only scanty bits of information about Delaney's and Kyra's life before the action of the novel sets in, we get to know important details about América's and Cándido's childhood, youth and the circumstances which make them seek their fortune in the U.S.A. In this way the reader will develop understanding and sympathy for the characters' motives of behavior.

9. Who do you think are the most interesting "minor" characters of the novel?

- José Navidad: an evil character among illegal Mexicans depicted in this way to avoid a black and white view of the groups of people involved
- Dom Flood: a super-rich, mysterious and criminal banker, confined to his house by an electronic shackle; he gives an extravagant party; he cunningly makes use of the infatuation of Kyra's mother in order to get rid of the shackle
- Jack Cherrystone: the voice of Hollywood resounding with xenophobic clichés
- Todd Sweet: a figure of sportive appearance; the only Arroyo Blanco resident who speaks out against their residential area being changed into a fortified community
- Al Lopez and Señor Willis: a contrast of Mexican-American builders
- the Oregon farmer: a figure of humanity
- the two American dudes who give their turkey to Cándido

10. Analyze in what ways the author's use of symbolism contributes to the meaning of the novel with reference to:

a) the coyote
b) borders, boundaries, fences, gate and wall
c) names

a) the coyote

- The coyote stands for Pre-Columbian America where it could roam its territories unhampered by European settlers. As with increasing urbanization its territory becomes encroached upon, it adapts to the changed conditions as an urban coyote which drinks water from swimming pools, eats pet food and even stalks and preys on small pets. With its amazing abilities to adjust it is fit for survival under changing and endangering circumstances.
- América identifies with the coyote; both regard man to be their common enemy; both are molested and persecuted by men (p. 179).
- The coyote is seen as an animal whose movements are not restricted by fences or walls; therefore the Mexican scouts who try to smuggle their countrymen through the Tortilla Curtain into the U.S.A. are called "coyotes".
- The coyote as the trickster and survivor in foreign territories may stand for the illegal Mexican in California in general: both show resourcefulness, never-ending energy and slyness to find a niche for survival, even if this might involve unlawful intrusion and stealing.

- Like a coyote Cándido scales the Arroyo Blanco wall to get what he needs there to build a shelter. Just as the Dinmont terriers are stalked and killed by a coyote, Cándido lures and kills Dame Edith, the Siamese cat, to have some food.
- José Navidad embodies the evil qualities of a coyote.

b) borders, boundaries, fences, gate and wall

- The Tortilla Curtain is to protect the rich U.S.A. from the poor and hungry Mexicans.
- The fence and the wall are to protect the Arroyo Blanco residents from the threat of illegal aliens and the crime coming with mass immigration in Southern California; at the same time residents hope to prevent coyotes from intruding into their housing areas.
- The wall guards the wealth and privileges of Americans against intruders.
- The Tortilla Curtain stands for the wall Americans erect in their minds to fend off illegal aliens or even immigrants altogether.
- The border of the Arroyo Blanco Estates represents the frontier between luxury settlement and nature giving Delaney the opportunity to oscillate between both.
- Kyra crosses the county border and at the same time transgresses into new professional territory (developing instead of selling).

c) names

In many cases the names selected hint at the dominant qualities of the characters or – in ironical reversal – at the absence or the opposite of them. For an overview of these meaningful names see p. 54.

11. Why do the residents of Arroyo Blanco increasingly develop xenophobia manifesting itself in the fortification of their community?

- fear of crime; a craving for safety in unsafe times
- fear of losing their privileged social position
- As in their view the politicians are unable to exercise efficient controls at the border, they feel forced to erect effective fortifications around their own territory; they feel entitled to make use of the right of self-protection.
- Confronted with the phenomenon of mass immigration they feel under siege; they want to start a backlash.
- They see their culture in danger when – in their eyes – uncivilized, uneducated, unskilled hordes swamp their territory.

12. "The true heroine of the novel is América". Discuss.

Pro

- She is only seventeen years old and has to cope with immense difficulties (she does not speak the language of the country, is dependent on a partner who displays macho behavior in spite of his temporary inability to earn a living for her).
- She patiently and expertly nurses Cándido to get well again.
- She is strong enough not to tell Cándido about the rape in order not to crush him in his male pride, his self-respect and his role as her protector.
- In spite of his massive resistance she has her way to look for work herself.
- She is clear-sighted enough to insist on her looking for work if they want to survive.
- She is strong enough to make Cándido realize her needs and her intense wish to stay at an apartment for one night at least.
- In spite of her youth, inexperience and lack of assistance she successfully gives birth to a baby.
- She loses her daughter in the flood, but saves her husband.
- ?

Con

- She is too moody and introverted.
- She is a representative of the Mexican attitude: "acquiesce, accept. Things would change, sure they would, but only if God willed it" (p. 172); this fatalistic attitude is expressed when Jim Shirley molests her; she should have hit back.
- ?

Creative Writing

13. Describe and characterize the ending of the novel. If the story were to be continued, what would you expect to happen?

The novel has a surprising and melodramatic happy ending. Furthermore, it is quite abrupt and open, in this way it makes a provoking appeal to the reader to speculate on alternative endings.
What do you expect to happen?

- ?
- Delaney revokes his racism, sees to it that Cándido gets a steady job with Al Lopez, forces Kyra to find an apartment for him and América, succeeds

in opening up the labor exchange at the lumber yard.
- Delaney hands the illegal Mexican couple over to the INS police.
- Cándido's story is taken up by the media and he is made a hero; with the money given to him by TV stations he buys a car and on Topanga Canyon Road bumps into Delaney injuring him badly.

14. Add a final passage to the given ending of the novel or write a differing ending of the novel starting with the mudslide.

15. Write a letter to a Hollywood producer trying to convince him to turn the novel into a movie.

Make use of the following arguments:
- Illegal immigration is a burning social issue in the U.S.A. and world-wide.
- The compassionate story with its powerful and moving ending may acquire the emotional appeal of the famous *Grapes of Wrath* movie.
- There is the spectacular scenery of the Santa Monica Mountains and the Pacific Coast.
- It gives four movie actors the opportunity of representing highly interesting characters.
- It is a straightforward narrative which can be easily changed into film action.
- The structure of the novel with its shifting scenes corresponds to film techniques.
- There are powerful climaxes; the tension in Part Three rises with the dramatic events.
- The natural disasters of fire and flood guarantee spectacular pictures.
- Because of T.C. Boyle's world-wide popularity the film will do extremely well at the box office.

16. Write a film script of the very last scene.

Sequence of scenes:
- Delaney, Cándido, and América in the floods of Topanga Creek
- América losing her grip on her little baby
- Delaney disappearing in the whirling water
- América stranded on the roof of the post office and helping Cándido to get up
- Cándido grasps the extended arm of … Delaney

B. Term Paper Ideas

- Gated Communities in California in fact and fiction: Arroyo Blanco compared with Hidden Hills
- Migrant Workers in California: from the "Bracero" Program to the day laborers of today
- The Mexican-American border: topography, border patrol, fortifications, the Tortilla Curtain, life in border cities
- How the Southwest was won: the Mexican-American war and the foundation of the Southwestern U.S. states
- The Spanish in Middle and North America: rise and fall of colonial rule
- Landmarks in immigration policy: 1965 Act – 1985 Amnesty Act – Proposition 187
- Los Angeles – a city of contrasts
- South California – a refuge of the very rich (e. g. Malibu, Santa Barbara)
- South California: natural beauty and natural disasters
- *The Tortilla Curtain* (T.C. Boyle) and *The Grapes of Wrath* (J. Steinbeck): the Mexican migrants as "the Okies" of our time
- Economic crises and population growth in Mexico (1970–2005) as push factors for Mexicans to leave their country
- Illegal workers in Germany – countries of origin, kinds of jobs, life in "the shadow"
- Study in the history of American Nativism: the Irish – the Chinese – the Mexicans
- The coyote: biological characterization – regional spread in North America – the "urban" coyote
- Hollywood and the American literary movie: *Gone with the Wind* – *The Grapes of Wrath* – *The Old Man and the Sea* – *To Kill a Mocking Bird* – *Snow Falling on Cedars* – *The Road to Wellville*. Select three examples.